Muhammad Ashfaq, Rashedul Hasan, Jošt Merčon
Central Bank Digital Currencies and the Global Financial System

Muhammad Ashfaq, Rashedul Hasan,
Jošt Merčon

Central Bank Digital Currencies and the Global Financial System

Theory and Practice

DE GRUYTER

ISBN 978-3-11-099607-4
e-ISBN (PDF) 978-3-11-098239-8
e-ISBN (EPUB) 978-3-11-098297-8

Library of Congress Control Number: 2023937998

Bibliographic information published by the Deutsche Nationalbibliothek
The Deutsche Nationalbibliothek lists this publication in the Deutsche Nationalbibliografie;
detailed bibliographic data are available on the internet at http://dnb.dnb.de.

© 2023 Walter de Gruyter GmbH, Berlin/Boston
Cover image: piranka/E+/Getty Images
Typesetting: Integra Software Services Pvt. Ltd.
Printing and binding: CPI books GmbH, Leck

www.degruyter.com

Muhammad Ashfaq
To my beloved and amazing wife, who has supported me beyond my imagination and to our wonderful kids Ahmad and Ayesha. Their support provided me immense motivation to write this book. I would like to also thank my parents for their immense prays.

Rashedul Hasan
To my beloved daughter, Maisrah Hasan and spouse, Tamiza Parveen, who have been my unwavering source of inspiration and support throughout the writing of this book. Your love, encouragement, and patience keeps me going. I dedicate this book to you as a token of my deepest appreciation and love. Thank you for being my constant inspiration and my greatest cheerleader.

Jošt Merčon
I dedicate this book to my family, friends, and colleagues, whose unwavering support and encouragement played an integral role in the successful completion of my master's studies, the writing of the master's thesis, and this book. I am deeply grateful for their patience, understanding, and belief in my ability to achieve my goals. Additionally, I am grateful to the professors of IU International University of Applied Sciences in Germany who challenged and inspired me to think critically and creatively about the complex topics of finance and accounting. Their guidance and mentorship were indispensable in bringing the master's thesis and this book to fruition.

Acknowledgments

Writing a book is not a solitary activity, and we have been fortunate to have the support and guidance of many individuals throughout this journey. We extend our sincere gratitude to every one of them.

First and foremost, we would like to thank De Gruyter for believing in this project and offering us the opportunity to share our ideas with a wider audience. We would like to thank Content Editor Lucy Jarman for the continuous support.

We greatly appreciate the feedback provided by Dr. Tariq Abbasi, Prof. Dr. Manuela Ender, and Dr. Stephen Foster on the earlier versions of this book. Moreover, we would also like to thank Prof. Dr. Florian Hummel, Prof. Dr. Victor J. Randall, Prof. Dr. Gerhard Sälzer, and Dr. Abdul Rauf for their motivation and relentless support.

We extend our heartfelt appreciation to Sarah Wasim for her excellent support in the preparation of this book. Finally, we also thank Ben Birdsall and the Wittenborg University of Applied Sciences for their generous support in proofreading and editing this book.

Thank you all for your contributions to this book.

https://doi.org/10.1515/9783110982398-202

Contents Overview

https://doi.org/10.1515/9783110982398-203

Contents

Preface

The way we communicate with one another and do business has been completely transformed by the usage of technology. The introduction of central bank digital currencies (CBDCs) is one of the most recent advances in this field of digital currency. The general public, financial institutions, and governments all across the world are interested in this new innovation.

This book, *Central Bank Digital Currencies and Global Financial System – Theory and Practice,* offers a thorough and in-depth investigation of the Central Bank Digital Currencies (CBDCs), examining their development, traits, and prospective effects on the global financial system. A wide range of viewpoints, from the technological features of cryptocurrencies to the regulatory and policy consequences of CBDCs, are covered in this book with the goal of providing a thorough theoretical basis and practical insights on the subject.

There are eight chapters in this book, each of which deals with a distinct facet of the subject. In the first chapter, we introduce FinTech and blockchain are introduced, their characteristics and international laws are covered, as well as cutting-edge uses for them, including smart contracts, open banking, and security tokens. The emergence of cryptocurrencies and digital currencies is covered in Chapter 2, along with their history, frameworks, and key benefits and drawbacks.

In Chapter 3, we cover the development of CBDCs along with its place in the current payment system. We also explore the potential involvement of customers, and financial institutions in the development of CBDCs. The adoption possibilities, potential currency substitutes, benefits, cybersecurity threats, and potential effects on financial inclusion are all covered in this chapter.

In Chapter 4, the concepts, legality, and practical distinctions between CBDCs and cryptocurrency in general are covered. A summary of the different CBDCs throughout the world, including the Sand Dollar, JAM-DEX, Dcash, digital ruble, the Bank of Korea's CBDC program, eNaira, Project Aber, digital euro, project icebreaker and project nexus is given in Chapter 5. We provide detailed discussion on the digital euro and digital yuan in Chapters 6 and 7, respectively. Finally, we end the book by providing future research directions and concluding remarks in Chapter 8.

Students, academics, and practitioners who want to comprehend the advantages and disadvantages of CBDCs and how they could affect the global financial system should read this book. Readers will be able to increase their knowledge and competence in this rapidly expanding field thanks to the book's diversified and all-encompassing approach.

We anticipate that this book will be an invaluable resource for the future study on central bank digital currencies and its implications across the globe.

https://doi.org/10.1515/9783110982398-205

1 Introduction of FinTech and Blockchain

> **Key facts of FinTech and Blockchain**
> - According to a report by PwC and CB Insights, global FinTech investment reached $134.5 billion in 2020, with the Asia-Pacific region accounting for the largest share of investment at 44% (PwC and CB Insights, 2020).
> - A report by Accenture estimates that blockchain technology could add $1.76 trillion to global gross domestic product (GDP) by 2030 (Accenture, 2020).
> - According to a report by the World Economic Forum, 10% of global GDP will be stored on blockchain technology by 2027 (World Economic Forum, 2018).
> - The smart contract market will grow from $1.2 billion in 2019 to $7.7 billion by 2024, at a compound annual growth rate (CAGR) of 44.5% (MarketsandMarkets, 2019).
> - According to a report by the World Bank, distributed ledger technology (DLT) could reduce the costs of cross-border payments by up to $15 billion per year (World Bank, 2019).
> - A report by the Cambridge Centre for Alternative Finance estimates that the number of blockchain wallets has grown from around 6.7 million in 2016 to over 42 million in 2019 (Cambridge Centre for Alternative Finance, 2019).

Introduction

Financial technology, or FinTech, is reshaping the financial services sector by providing cutting-edge solutions that alter how customers and businesses interact with money and debt. FinTech firms are at the vanguard of this revolution, introducing cutting-edge products and services that are upending the conventional banking industry.

Blockchain technology is one of the most important developments in the FinTech industry. A decentralized digital database called the blockchain enables secure peer-to-peer transactions without the aid of middlemen like banks. A wide range of businesses, including finance, supply chain management, and healthcare, are already utilizing block chain technology.

Ripple is an illustration of a blockchain-based FinTech business that makes use of technology to help financial institutions make quick, safe, and affordable cross-border payments. Another illustration is Circle, a FinTech firm that created the USD Coin (USDC) stablecoin, which enables blockchain-based cross-border payments, remittances, and trading. USDC is fixed to the value of the US dollar.

The application of machine learning (ML) and artificial intelligence (AI) is another area where FinTech is having a significant impact. Banks and other financial institutions can make better decisions by using these tools to analyze financial data, spot trends, and make predictions. Roostify, a FinTech firm, is one illustration. Roostify employs AI and ML to speed up the mortgage application process for borrowers.

In general, FinTech is reshaping the future of financial services by bringing new technology and services that are accelerating, securing, and streamlining financial

https://doi.org/10.1515/9783110982398-001

transactions. The financial services sector is about to undergo a significant shift as a result of the emergence of blockchain and other disruptive technologies.

FinTech

In the early 2000s, many traditional banks were operating as global banks, but the majority of them were uncertain about digitalization. As a result, they put little effort into researching digitalization. On the other hand, there was a rapid growth of newly developed start-ups that saw the potential of using digitalization in combination with traditional banks' business models to offer new digital products and services for the financial sector. These new developments are being recognized as financial technology, or FinTech, for short. There is a diverse range of definitions available to define FinTech; however, Gupta and Tham (2018) describe the word FinTech as any kind of start-up that uses some level of technology to create a financial product or service. There are two kinds of FinTech start-ups: one providing tech-enabled financial services; and the other providing novel solutions.

In recent years, due to the rapid advancement of smartphone technology, FinTech has become more customer-centric. FinTech consists of retail banking solutions, fundraising, education and investment management, and the development and support of cryptocurrencies. Although cryptocurrencies may be the best-known segment of FinTech in the public eye, the most lucrative part of this is connected to retail banking solutions. Kagan divides it further into four segments:
- Tools that support money transfers
- Start-up or investment money-raising
- Applying for credit
- Other services that are used to perform individually at the level of financial institutions

EYGM Limited developed the FinTech Adoption Index in 2019 which indicates that one-third of consumers regularly utilize at least two or more FinTech services. Putting the numbers into context, according to PwC (2021), funding of FinTech has risen 40% and reached a total amount of $17.6 billion, as shown in Figure 1.1. Therefore, immense growth has put FinTech in the top spot of emerging areas by the number of total investments.

FinTech companies operate under the concept of unbundling the services that traditional banks tend to offer under one roof to their customers via smartphone apps or web platforms. Traditional banks have, in recent years, started to pay more attention to the FinTech industry and have started to invest in companies that tend to disrupt the finance industry. However, will the increase in investment into the FinTech sector be enough for traditional banks to catch up? In our opinion, they need, alongside

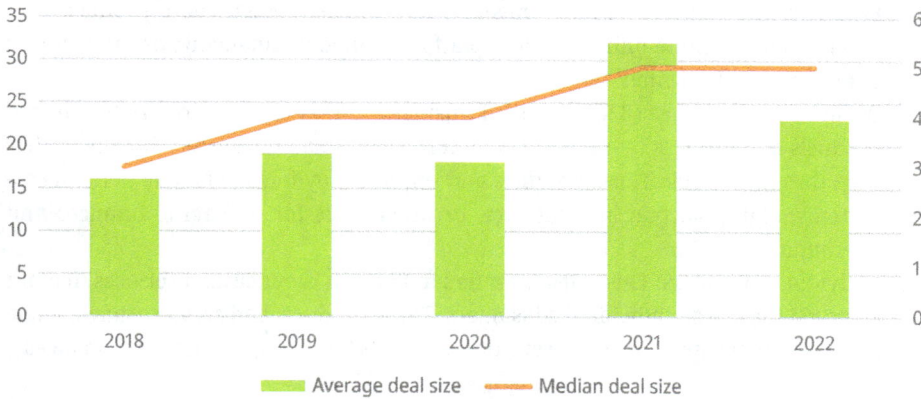

Figure 1.1: Annual FinTech funding and deals in the EU.
Note: *All figures are in millions of US dollars*
Source: CB Insights (2022)

investment into established FinTech companies, to develop solutions of their own to stay competitive in the fast-changing field of banking and finance.

The current most significant users of FinTech products and services can be diverse. Kagan divided FinTech users into four categories, as depicted in Figure 1.2.

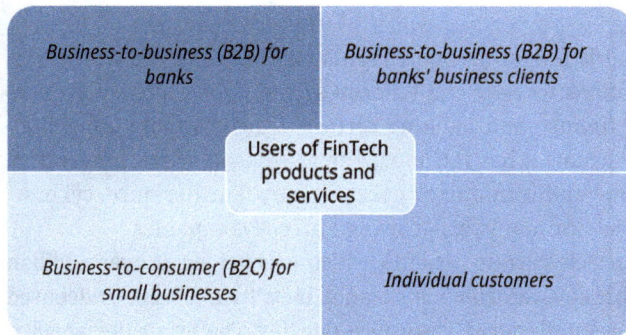

Figure 1.2: Users of FinTech products and services.
Source: Kegan (2020)

–   Business-to-business (B2B) for banks: This category refers to FinTech products and services that are intended for use by banks themselves, rather than by individual consumers or small businesses. These products and services may include technology for back-office operations, risk management, or compliance.
–   Business-to-business (B2B) for banks' business clients: This category refers to FinTech products and services that are intended for use by the business clients of

banks, such as small and medium-sized enterprises (SMEs). These products and services may include online lending platforms, invoice financing, or other forms of alternative financing.

– Business-to-consumer (B2C) for small businesses: This category refers to FinTech products and services that are intended for use by small businesses directly, rather than through a bank. These products and services may include mobile point-of-sale systems, digital accounting software, or other tools for managing finances and operations.

– Individual customers: This category refers to FinTech products and services that are intended for use by individual consumers. These products and services may include mobile banking apps, robo-advisers, or other tools for managing personal finances.

The FinTech industry focuses on youth. Younger users are more aware of FinTech and are likely to use FinTech solutions and products more. Therefore, consumer-oriented FinTech aims primarily towards the millennial generation, representing the most significant earning potential for FinTech start-ups. For business clients, the aim is to offer traditional banking and financing services online or via smartphone applications. This means that customers are not required to visit the bank in person anymore, as financing or establishing a card payment system can be secured online.

FinTech Regulations Across the Globe

As the financial services field is one of the most regulated sectors in the world, it is worth observing how regulations work in the FinTech sector. When technologies intersect with the traditional finance and banking sectors, it brings many new challenges for regulators. In particular, it has introduced new kinds of crime prevention, such as preventing cybercrime and introducing cybersecurity. Furthermore, cybersecurity is now a regulatory issue for many fast-growing FinTech companies.

San Francisco-based insurtech start-up Zenefits, which was valued at over a billion dollars in private markets, broke California's insurance laws by allowing unlicensed brokers to sell its products and underwrite insurance policies. The Securities and Exchange Commission (SEC) fined the firm $980,000 and they had to pay $7 million to the California Department of Insurance.

In service- and product-oriented FinTech companies, the regulation issue is even more significant in the world of cryptocurrencies as this part of FinTech was not regulated at all until the end of 2020. Crypto coin developers use initial coin offerings (ICOs) as their fundraising method, which allows them to raise funds directly from investors. ICOs are still unregulated in most countries, which is incredibly attractive for scams and frauds.

Several governments have tried to stop such fraudulent acts and have implemented various existing regulations to make them applicable to the FinTech industry. However, these are usually not entirely successful. More successful ones have been implementing FinTech regulatory sandboxes, which were set up to study and evaluate the implications of regulations and technologies in the sector. One of the successful outcomes of regulatory sandboxes is represented by the EU where the European Commission passed Regulation (EU) 2016/679 of the European Parliament and of the Council of 27 April 2016. This regulations was issued for the protection of natural persons with regard to the processing of personal data and on the free movement of such data. This regulation repeals the Directive 95/46/EC (the General Data Protection Regulation, or GDPR for short).

The regulation of FinTech differs by nation and area, with some governments adopting a more progressive stance while others are still working out how to deal with the industry's explosive growth and innovation. The Payment Services Directive 2 (PSD2) has been put into effect in the European Union to offer a unified legal framework for FinTech businesses operating in the EU. Federal and state laws in the United States are inconsistent, with some states offering progressive regulatory frameworks for FinTech firms than others. Other nations, including the United Kingdom, Singapore, China, India, and Canada, have created regulatory sandboxes and published guidelines for a variety of FinTech applications, including mobile banking, digital payments, and digital and online banking. We provide a brief summary of FinTech regulations across the globe below and outline the institutions in Table 1.1.

North America
- United States: Due to the patchwork of state and federal legislation, FinTech regulation in the US is complicated. The Federal Reserve and the Consumer Financial Protection Bureau are two federal organizations that regulate various facets of FinTech. While other states have not yet done so, others, like New York and California, have formed their own regulatory frameworks for FinTech companies.
- Canada: Although it differs by province, the regulatory climate for FinTech in Canada is thought to be relatively progressive. Among the organizations in charge of overseeing FinTech in Canada are the Financial Consumer Agency of Canada (FCAC) and the Office of the Superintendent of Financial Institutions (OSFI).

Europe
- United Kingdom: The UK (United Kingdom) has one of the most forward-thinking regulatory environments in the world for FinTech. For FinTech companies to test their goods and services in a regulated setting, the Financial Conduct Authority (FCA) has set up a regulatory sandbox. The UK government has also launched several programs to aid FinTech businesses, including the FinTech Alliance.

- Germany: The Federal Financial Supervisory Authority (BaFin) is in charge of regulating the FinTech sector in Germany, where the government has mostly stayed out of the way. For a number of FinTech applications, including crowdfunding and digital banking, BaFin has released guidelines.
- France: The regulatory landscape in France is rather progressive for FinTech firms. The main FinTech regulator in France is the Autorité des Marchés Financiers (AMF), which has created a regulatory sandbox where FinTech businesses can test their goods and services in a safe setting.
- Italy: The Bank of Italy (BOI) serves as the country's primary FinTech regulatory body. For a number of FinTech applications, including digital banking and payments, the BOI has released rules. Additionally, the BOI has created a regulatory sandbox for FinTech firms.
- Spain: The primary FinTech regulator in Spain is the Bank of Spain (BOS). The BOS has published recommendations for a number of FinTech subfields, including digital banking and payments. Additionally, the BOS has created a regulatory sandbox for FinTech.
- The Netherlands: The primary FinTech regulator in the Netherlands is the Dutch central bank, De Nederlandsche Bank (DNB). For a number of FinTech applications, including digital banking and payments, the DNB has released rules. Additionally, the DNB has created a regulatory sandbox for FinTech firms.

Asia
- Singapore: The FinTech regulatory landscape in Singapore is seen as being quite forward thinking. A regulatory sandbox for FinTech companies has been developed by the Monetary Authority of Singapore (MAS), along with a number of other initiatives to encourage the development of the FinTech sector.
- China: China has strong regulations in place for specific FinTech sectors, such as internet lending, and takes a more heavy-handed approach to FinTech regulation. Among the organizations in charge of overseeing FinTech in China are the People's Bank of China (PBOC) and the China Banking and Insurance Regulatory Commission (CBIRC).
- India: The Reserve Bank of India (RBI) serves as the country's primary FinTech regulatory body. A regulatory sandbox for FinTech start-ups has been formed by the RBI, and it has also released a variety of recommendations for several FinTech subfields like mobile payments and digital lending.

Africa
- South Africa: To allow FinTech companies to test their goods and services in a regulated setting, the South African Reserve Bank (SARB) has set up a regulatory sandbox. The SARB has also released rules for a number of FinTech subfields, including digital payments and banking.

- Nigeria: The primary FinTech regulator in Nigeria is the Central Bank of Nigeria (CBN). For numerous FinTech applications, including mobile banking and e-payment services, the CBN has released rules.
- Kenya: The primary FinTech regulator in Kenya is the Central Bank of Kenya (CBK). The CBK has created a regulatory sandbox for FinTech businesses and has released guidelines for a number of FinTech subfields, including mobile banking and online lending.

South America
- Brazil: The primary FinTech regulator in Brazil is the Central Bank of Brazil (BCB). For a number of FinTech applications, including crowdfunding and digital payments, the BCB has released rules.
- Chile: FinTech in Chile is primarily regulated by the Central Bank of Chile (BCCh). The BCCh has created a regulatory sandbox for FinTech businesses and has released rules for a number of FinTech subfields, including digital payments and banking.

Middle East
- United Arab Emirates: The Central Bank of the United Arab Emirates (CBUAE) is the primary FinTech regulator in the UAE. The CBUAE has created a regulatory sandbox for FinTech businesses and has released guidelines for a number of FinTech subfields, including digital banking and payments.
- Saudi Arabia: The primary FinTech regulator in Saudi Arabia is the Saudi Arabian Central Bank(SAMA). The SAMA has created a regulatory sandbox for FinTech businesses and has released rules for a number of FinTech subfields, including digital banking and payments.

Innovative Application in the FinTech Sector

There are many potentials uses for FinTech that were made possible with the introduction of blockchain technology. Some applications and products are specifically designed for a single customer, while others are developed for broader use. Figure 1.3 indicates some of the most promising, widely discussed, and useful applications in the FinTech sector that have been developed the furthest and are already in use by consumers and businesses.

Table 1.1: Key regulatory institutions governing FinTech firms.

Country	Regulatory Institution	Abbreviation
United States	The Federal Reserve and the Consumer Financial Protection Bureau	CFPB
Canada	Financial Consumer Agency of Canada	FCAC
	Office of the Superintendent of Financial Institutions	OSFI
United Kingdom	Financial Conduct Authority	FCA
Germany	Federal Financial Supervisory Authority	BaFin
France	Autorité des Marchés Financiers	AMF
Italy	Bank of Italy	BOI
Spain	Bank of Spain	BOS
The Netherlands	De Nederlandsche Bank	DNB
Singapore	Monetary Authority of Singapore	MAS
China	People's Bank of China	PBOC
	China Banking and Insurance Regulatory Commission	CBIRC
India	Reserve Bank of India	RBI
South Africa	South African Reserve Bank	SARB
Nigeria	Central Bank of Nigeria	CBN
Kenya	Central Bank of Kenya	CBK
Brazil	Central Bank of Brazil	BCB
Chile	Central Bank of Chile	BCCh
United Arab Emirates	Central Bank of the United Arab Emirates	CBUAE
Saudi Arabia	Saudi Arabian Central bank	SAMA

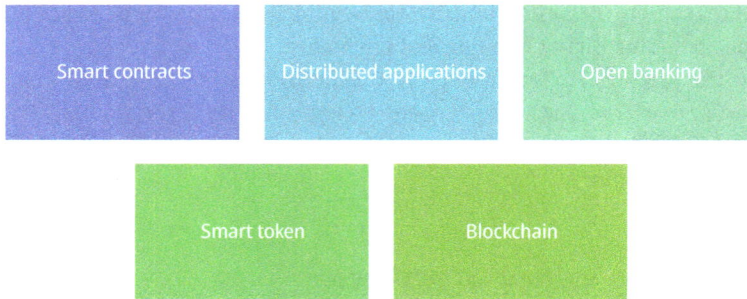

Figure 1.3: Innovative application in the FinTech sector.

Smart Contracts

Smart contracts are one of the innovations enabled by blockchain technology. One definition of a smart contract, developed by Gopie (2018) and published by IBM, defines it as "a line of code stored in a blockchain that begins to operate independently once certain conditions are met." The advantages of smart contracts are seen in business collaborations where contracts and agreements are necessary, as they eliminate the need for intermediaries like lawyers.

Smart contracts are a type of Ethereum account that have a balance and can send transactions over the network but are not controlled by a user. Instead, they are deployed to the network and run as programmed. Users can interact with smart contracts by submitting transactions that execute a function defined on the contract. Smart contracts can define rules and automatically enforce them through code. Figure 1.4 provides an indication of the volatility in the Ethereum daily prices.

Ethereum's price history suggests that it was worth significantly less in 2022 than during late 2021, although nowhere near the lowest price recorded. This was due to technological developments such as the Berlin upgrade and the Ethereum Merge, which reduced ETH gas prices and reduced transaction fees. Ethereum's future and the decentralized finance (DeFi) industry are tied to this industry, as Ethereum is technically not a currency but an open-source software platform for blockchain applications, with Ether being the cryptocurrency that is used inside the Ethereum network. Non-fungible tokens (NFTs) are the best-known applications of Ethereum NFTs, with the market cap of NFTs worldwide growing nearly ten-fold between 2018 and 2020.

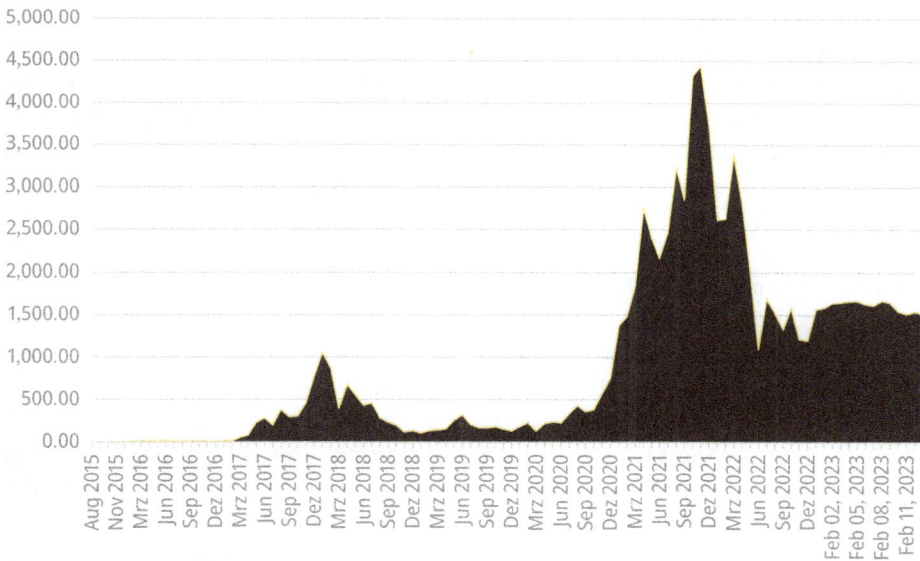

Figure 1.4: Ethereum (ETH) price chart.
Source: CoinGecko (2023)

Smart contracts are primarily similar to regular contracts but have some advantages over them. For example, buying a new car through financing often involves several companies, takes a few days, and involves several parties, each of which takes a considerable amount of time to prepare documentation and charges the customer for their services, adding to the cost of the car. Smart contracts can streamline this process and reduce costs by eliminating intermediaries and automating the process. Additionally, smart contracts are automated and completely digital, which makes them faster and more accurate than traditional contracts and can also increase trust in transactions.

While the number of smart contracts has increased in recent years, it is believed that they have the potential to fundamentally change how parties conduct contracts in the future. However, there is still room for developing smart contracts before they become adopted widely across various industries. Levi and Lipton (2018) conclude that true revolution of smart contracts may come from paradigms that have yet to be imagined.

It is worth noting that while smart contracts have the potential to revolutionize the way we conduct business and legal agreements, it is important to consider the legal and regulatory implications surrounding the use of smart contracts. They may not be recognized as legally binding by certain jurisdictions and laws may need to be adapted to accommodate this new technology. Additionally, the use of smart contracts may also raise issues related to data privacy and security. Therefore, it is essential to consult with legal and regulatory experts to ensure compliance with relevant laws and regulations before implementing smart contracts.

In summary, smart contracts are a promising innovation enabled by blockchain technology that can streamline the process of conducting business and legal agreements, increase trust and security, and reduce costs. However, it is important to consider the legal and regulatory implications and ensure compliance before implementing them. As technology continues to evolve, it will be interesting to see how smart contracts will shape the future of legal agreements and business transactions.

Distributed Applications

Distributed applications (ĐApps) operate on a separate platform from smart contracts. Smart contracts operate on cloud computing platforms and can operate on several computers at once. Unlike traditional applications which run on a single dedicated machine, ĐApps connect with other participants to carry out a certain task. It allows users to collaborate, access, edit, and exchange applications through cloud computing servers or client-server networks.

In the FinTech sector, the term "app" is frequently used in conjunction with blockchain technology to integrate apps into work processes. This provides a tool for better transparency to satisfy regulatory obligations. Additionally, ĐApps can eliminate or reduce the need for intermediaries in transactions and give customers access to peer-to-peer lending and cryptocurrencies. In the future, these apps may potentially be used as a means of identifying and validating previous blockchain transactions in order to enable open banking.

Open Banking

Open banking, which has already been developed to some extent, can be further extended with the help of blockchain and ÐApps. According to Estevez (2020), open banking is a type of banking that allows third-party financial services providers open access to consumer banking, transaction, and other financial data from banks and non-bank financial institutions through the use of application programming interfaces (APIs). In the future, open banking will make it possible for organizations to share data and account information. Consumers, financial institutions, and outside service providers will all be able to make use of such data.

For example, a consumer could easily switch checking accounts from one bank to another with the use of an open banking system. According to Open Banking Europe (2021), this process could take place in a matter of seconds as opposed to the lengthy procedure currently in use. Additionally, open banking could assist customers who wish to purchase a property by gathering information and offering financial advice on what they can afford. However, open banking may also give lenders access to precise information about a consumer's financial situation and related risks, enabling them to create the most advantageous loan conditions. If fully realized, open banking can become the biggest breakthrough in the financial sector in the current era.

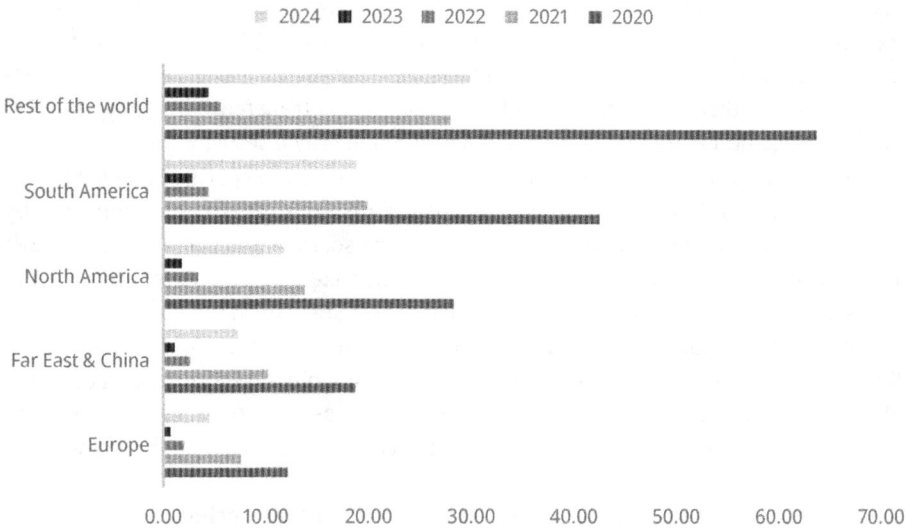

Figure 1.5: Open banking users across regions.
Note: *All figures are in millions*
Source: Juniper Research (2021)

Figure 1.5 indicates that the number of open banking users worldwide is expected to grow at an average annual rate of nearly 50% between 2020 and 2024, with the European market being the largest. As the graph shows, in 2020, Europe counted approximately 12.2 million open banking users. This figure is expected to reach 63.8 million by 2024. As of 2020, 24.7 million individuals worldwide used open banking services, a number that is forecast to reach 132.2 million by 2024.

Security Tokens

After Liechtenstein Parliament passed the Token and Trusted Technology Service Provider Act (TVTG) on 3 October 2020, security tokens have gained a lot of attention. The act states security token to be a token which is a digital representation of information on a telegraphic transfer (TT) system. The token can represent claims or membership rights vis-à-vis a person, rights to property or other rights. However, it can also be "empty," meaning that no rights are represented by the token. Pure virtual currencies without any reference to real assets are an example of this.

A security token is a financial instrument that grants the owner the rights to ownership and a portion of the token's future revenues. The token can be portrayed as a portion of ownership in a piece of real estate, a classic car, an original work of art, or more well-known assets like bonds and other debt securities. Security tokens are governed as securities by some regulators. Security tokens are treated in the same way as regular securities. They stand for a pledge to give their owner a portion of any future cash flow. If the three requirements of European law – transferability, negotiability, and standardization – are met, issuers are permitted to create security tokens.

Majaski (2020) defines another alternative definition of security tokens. She defines it as a "portable device that authenticates a person's identity electronically by storing some sort of personal information." By doing so, the owner of a security token can gain access to a network server by entering the token's credentials into the computer system. A variety of media devices can store security tokens. Some of them might be hardware tokens that are stored on USB devices or included in chipsets. Additionally, Bluetooth and wireless alternatives are available. A security token as a concrete illustration of online banking where an additional layer of security is required to secure the account. A security token in the form of a USB stick holding a security token is required to access such an account.

Security tokens can be applied in a variety of situations, including those where ordinary securities are used. For example, practically all traded assets may be tokenized under the Liechtenstein Blockchain Act. This implies that investors may acquire a portion of a classic car, or a work of art. Security token offerings (STOs) are also made possible by the introduction of security tokens. Collet et al. (2020) describe STOs as a "process where a financial security is issued in the form of a digital asset."

Therefore, an issued digital asset represents the right of partial ownership in the issuing company and/or its asset. STOs are a completely different process to initial coin offerings (ICOs), which result in utility tokens.

STOs offer the following key advantages. With the use of smart contracts, all contract details are embedded into the token itself. As STOs are electronic, the documentation and regulatory processes are quicker and less time-consuming. Additionally, it is much simpler for parties and authorities to exchange documents.

All admission and trade procedures are automated, enabling a more streamlined and automated process. This may also lead to fewer mistakes. It is likely that in the future, security tokens will lead to less expensive and quicker initial security offerings and will also establish automated and more standardized processes in terms of regulations.

Distributed Ledger Technology

Distributed ledger technology (DLT) is one of the fundamental technologies that was created long before the FinTech industry flourished. It is still frequently used today and supports a variety of FinTech goods and services. The definition of DLT is viewed differently by many researchers and organizations, and they also construct them with various perspectives and usability goals. On the one hand, some definitions describe a specific component of DLT, while others reflect a more general aspect. Some definitions are particularly narrow in their focus and observation. As a result, no consensus on a common definition exists yet. To comprehend many facets, development strategies, characteristics, and usefulness of various forms of DLT, it is imperative to observe several definitions.

According to Gradstein et al. (2017), DLT is a cutting-edge technology that enables an innovative, disruptive approach to data recording and sharing that is rapidly evolving. It operates across numerous data repositories, or ledgers (journals). A distributed network of computer servers manages each ledger, which is made up of the same data record (nodes).

DLT is a technology that enables users to store and retrieve data in accordance with a certain set of assets and their holders in a shared database, according to Pinna and Ruttenberg (2016) of the European Central Bank (ECB). They create three hypothetical futures for DLTs. The first idea focuses on maintaining the fundamental ideas and principles of the company while implementing DLT to increase the company's productivity. The second notion is based on the deployment of DLT.

On the other hand, Tasca and Tessone (2018) define DLT from a different standpoint. They have come up with three key features that may be unique to DLT systems.

They describe it as a "community consensus-based distributed ledger where the storage of data is not based on chains of blocks." DLT is based on the following three principles:

- decentralization of consensus,
- transparency, and
- security and immutability.

Similarly, Benos et al. (2017) from the Bank of England uses Tasca and Tessone's definition of DLT, which bases the DLT system's description on a set of three features. DLT is a distributed database, in the sense that each node has a synchronized copy of the data," but it moves away from traditional distributed databases in three ways: decentralization, reliability in trust-less environments, cryptographic encryption.

The Frameworks of DLT

To discuss the benefits of distributed ledger technology, it is crucial to understand that DLT is not just a stand-alone technology. Similar to its definitions, several different DLT frameworks may distinguish and include various blockchains and DLTs. Many of these are still in development, and due to various demands, their designs may change. Platt's (2017) two dimensions are based on:
- DLT data diffusion model (global vs. local): This model predicts that DLTs would perform best in contexts where there are plenty of transactions between unrelated, dispersed organizations that have mutual trust. DLTs are developed to be highly scalable and can achieve a high level of confidentiality. On the other hand, some people may not be able to implement them due to their operational complexity.
- The functionality of the ledger system (stateful vs. stateless): The usefulness of ledgers tends to be restricted in stateless systems. Bitcoin operates on a stateless system that most closely resembles its initial form. Despite its stateless structure and original tools appearing difficult, Bitcoin could be considered essential. Its sole purpose is to create new Bitcoins gained from mining and deliver those coins to another public address. The on-chain functionality of stateful systems, as opposed to stateless systems, is greater and can include smart contracts or chain code. Ethereum is the best-known cryptocurrency that employs stateful protocols, and it is powered by the Ethereum Virtual Machine (EVM). With an oracle service acting as support to collect input from the real world, a stateful system enables its players to develop practically any functionality directly on DLT.

Glaser (2017), similar to Platt, divides the DLT framework into two different layers: the fabric layer and the application layer.
- The fabric layer is centralized in control, meaning that such fabric layers have complete control over every system that is functioning. For example, if a specific firm creates a fabric layer system and the code base is not open source, the entire fabric layer system is owned by the company. On the other hand, if the code is open

source, it will be harder to create and maintain. The fabric layer only provides necessary services.

– The application layer, on the other hand, allows the code to be written, changed, and maintained by any participant in the system. The code is in control of the participant who initially wrote a part of the code, and this control is also distributed among the participants who created parts of the code. Developers of the fabric layer have no control over the top of the system within the application layer because the system is open source; once it is online, other participants start to change and contribute their parts of the code.

The Distributed Nature of the Ledger

The distributive ledger is most evident in a peer-to-peer network, which allows self-interested users to record verifiable data in specific ledgers without relying on a central entity. With the absence of a trusted central party, speed can be increased while transaction costs can be greatly reduced or eliminated. Maintenance inefficiencies associated with the ledger and subsequent reconciliations can also be eliminated. From a security perspective, it is important to note that the use of DLT can greatly improve security due to the distributed nature of the ledger as there is no longer a single point of attack in a network.

The Consensus Mechanism

The distributive ledger is used to determine whether a specific transaction is legitimate or not. It is necessary for DLT to function correctly and uses a predefined, cryptographic validation specifically designed for the distributed ledger. The consensus process is also intended to detect and resolve conflicts between multiple competing entries, which are typically separate transactions presented by the same node. It corrects transaction sequences, prevents them from being hijacked by bad actors, and protects DLT against double-spend issues.

The Cryptographic Mechanisms

The cryptographic mechanisms are important components of DLT, particularly when DLT is used for blockchain applications. A cryptographic hash function is applied to each new data transaction or entry. It accepts any data size as input and computes a unique digital identifier or fingerprint (similar to a person's fingerprint) that can never be reproduced or changed under any circumstances. Its alteration can only be done if its data is altered.

Hashing adds a unique timestamp to the original data, along with the fingerprint. The result of hashing is a digest of a specified length, which appears to be completely unrelated and random when compared to the data or original input.

However, it is deterministic in nature, which means that there is a very low chance of the same value being determined for a different data input. The hashed data is then bundled into a transaction block, which can include any number of data sets, but is usually limited to a fixed size. These transaction blocks are signed with a digital signature, which uses public-key cryptography. This is a standard mechanism used in other applications such as HTTPS authentication protocols and payment card technologies. In many countries, digital signatures are widely recognized by law and banking laws as a replacement for physical signatures.

Each network participant has a private key, which is only known by its user and is used to sign digital messages or documents. The public key, however, can be seen by anyone and is used to locate and identify the recipient of the digital message as well as to identify and validate the sender of the message.

The Concept of DLT

To present DLT in an organized manner, it is best to describe the two most opposing ideas. Differentiation in two groups of DLT concepts comprise of:
- the set of data held by an individual network node,
- the set of data held in common by most nodes.

The key terms used in the Rauchs et al. (2018) conceptual framework are transaction, log, record, journal, and ledger (see Figure 1.6).

Figure 1.6: Conceptual framework of DLT.
Source: Rauchs et al. (2018)

In detail, Rauchs et al. (2018) describe them as:
- A transaction is described as any type of change to a ledger; however, it is not necessary that the change must be economic. Before a transaction takes place, it is called a proposed transaction or ledger entry, as the ledger has not yet approved it.
- A log is represented as a node that has been fully validated. It stores unconfirmed transactions or ledger entries in its mempool or log. Differences may occur between different logs.

- A record is first known as a candidate record. After approval from the network, it becomes a complete record, which is in line with network consensus rules. To clear approval, it is necessary to perform steps specified by the network protocol.
- A journal is the set of records mentioned above held by a node; however, those nodes may not be the same, and their consensus may differ. Therefore, journals can be partial, provisional, or heterogeneous and may not consist of identical records.
- A ledger is globally known as the authoritative set of records which represents the state in which the DLT system exists. It is taken from the convergence of synchronized individual journals.

The ledger concept is based on the example of Bitcoin. In the essence of Bitcoin, a transaction can be a way to transfer an asset from one user to another. The goal of the DLT system is to synchronize individual entries or journals of the DLT's structure which leads to "a convergence towards a single accepted set of authoritative records (the ledger)." With the sync of journals, the consensus of different parties that have not established or gained trust can reach over a shared data set. Moreover, in traditional centralized financial systems, involved participants do not need to rely on a central authority. Rauchs et al. (2018) believe that: "Conceptually, the 'ledger' should be regarded as a latent, abstract construct that is generated by the DLT system as a whole through the constant efforts of synchronizing the individual copies maintained by each full participant."

The relations between journals, nodes, and the decentralized ledger are visually described in Figure 1.7. It can be seen how each node of the DLT system can receive, validate, and process data. Furthermore, the yellow line represents the connections of different journals that are constantly in sync. A set of such nodes and journals forms a shared set of authoritative records combined into a ledger. Overall, the organization that develops and manages shared data results in the ledger which is the core of all DLT systems.

Similarly, Gradstein et al. (2017) describe the fundamentals of the ledger concept as a correlation of three frameworks which were described in the previous section (distributed nature of the ledger, consensus mechanism, and cryptographic mechanisms). Gradstei elaborate that the set of data is recorded in transaction blocks which are represented in chronological order (timestamp) and added to the ledger (blockchain).

Gradstein emphasize the importance of data which needs a proof of work and a digital signature of the sender's private key hash and the recipient's public key to conduct the transaction. The first entry, "the genesis block," which sets the timestamp and chronological order that other blocks will follow. Therefore, each block has its own unique timestamp. The terminology for this would be a "proof-of-work" protocol, which defines the block's position in the blockchain. Such a block and a series of hashed digests of transaction information cannot be altered after being integrated onto the blockchain.

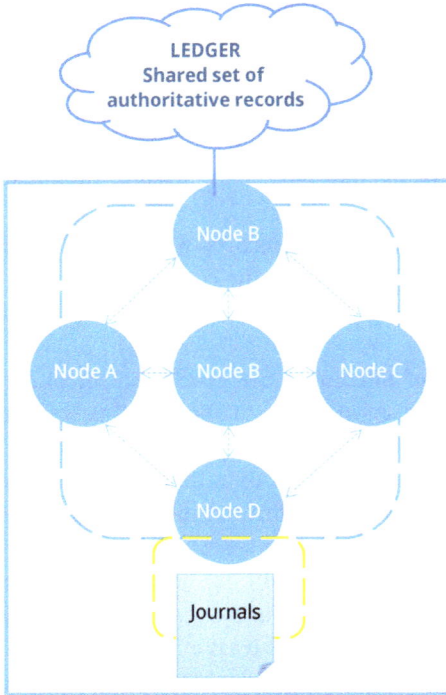

Figure 1.7: Depicting the ledger concept.
Source: Settipalli et al. (2023)

Gradstein, Krause, and Natarajan (2017) further describe blockchain as an example where certain blocks represent the last addition to the chain and, therefore, update the ledger. Once the block is added to the chain, it cannot subsequently be changed. Moreover, the block cannot be removed or deleted without gaining the consensus of all the individual blocks in the chain. Blockchain grows more significant, and it becomes harder to gain consensus from every block as the blocks are constantly generated and added to the chain. With each new addition, the whole network or blockchain gets updated, and also, all individual blocks receive an updated copy of the entire blockchain. Therefore, with the high speed of the newly added block, it is virtually impossible to gain consensus from all the different nodes in the chain and retroactively alter the blocks.

Connection of DLT and Blockchain

The development of DLT has been strongly linked to the development of cryptocurrencies. At present, the best-known cryptocurrency, Bitcoin, uses DLT as its underlying technology. A new form of DLT was described in the white paper published under the pseudonym Satoshi Nakamoto, which originated the concept of Bitcoin. The paper

(Nakamoto, 2008) described the vision for an electronic payment system which relies on trust.

Blockchain technology was developed as a result of the development of Bitcoin and DLT. It was designed to solve the double-spending problem in digital currencies. By overcoming this problem, it enabled the full development of digital money, similar to the digital transformations of email, cloud technology, and music.

In the case of Bitcoin, blockchain was developed to anonymize digital currency and make it free from government control and regulation; the identities of its users would also be hidden (Nakamoto, 2008). Bitcoin was the first cryptocurrency to be developed using DLT and blockchain, and it has been able to achieve a larger scale. It is believed that the potential of such technologies goes beyond digital currency and will be explored in the following sections.

Blockchain

Blockchain is a type of distributed ledger. Gradstein further describe how DLTs work, record, and synchronize changes in their electronic ledgers, compared to storing them in one centralized ledger, as was done in the past. Gradstein describe blockchain as a platform that organizes data into blocks which are connected or "chained" together. Blockchain was designed within DLT and maintained by anonymous users without establishing trust between them.

Conway (2020) describes blockchain as complicated and complex but its basic concept may prove to be relatively simple. Blockchain is based on the database concept which is an electronically stored information collection. Such databases and data are usually stored in a table format that allows for easier sorting, filtering and finding information, and specific data. Databases are usually designed to store a significant amount of data, which can be accessed and changed by many participants at the same time. Data can also be saved locally. To make it accessible to many participants simultaneously, companies usually store such data on servers which are powered by powerful computers. As a result, data is kept online where it may be accessed and synced by many users at once. A database can do multiple operations at once because of the computing power provided by storing data on servers.

As soon as a new transaction is added to a system, the blockchain-based transaction process begins. After entering, the transaction is transmitted to a server of decentralized peer-to-peer computers that are stationed all around the globe. Hereafter, the transaction goes onto a decentralized server, where a peer-to-peer computer network confirms it by conducting complex calculations. Once the transaction is confirmed, it is put into blocks with other transactions all together.

These blocks have a limited storage capacity of information. When the block limit is reached, it is chained onto a previously filled block, which forms a chain of data called the blockchain. When the later block is filled, which likewise adds to the chain, newly added information is compiled in it. A distinct timestamp is assigned to each freshly formed block that is chained onto the blockchain; this timestamp cannot be changed or removed. As indicated in Figure 1.8, since 2014, the Bitcoin market experienced exponential growth with megabytes growing by nearly one gigabyte every few days. The Bitcoin blockchain is a distributed database that contains a continuously growing and tamper-evident list of all Bitcoin transactions and records since the date of its initial release in January of 2009.

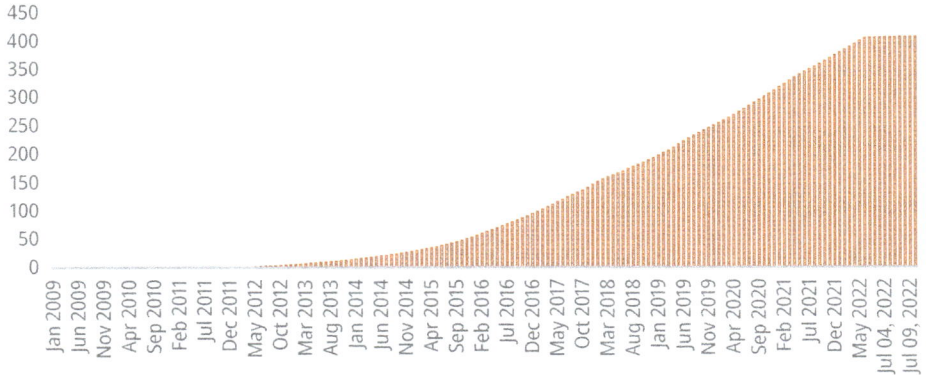

Figure 1.8: Size of the Bitcoin market 2009–2022.
Source: Blockchain.com (2023)

The Benefits and Drawbacks of Blockchain

Blockchain is the underlying technology of cryptocurrencies and other digital assets. As such, it is closely related to traditional banks and the global finance sector. To gain a better understanding of how blockchain differs from traditional banking, we will compare blockchain-based transactions to traditional banking transactions. Furthermore, we will see the differences between the two sectors and compare the benefits and drawbacks of blockchain to traditional banking. Conway (2020) compares key characteristics between a typical bank and a cryptocurrency based on the blockchain. We present the major advantages and disadvantages of blockchain below.

Benefits

– Accessibility: The first advantage of blockchain is that it is open 24 hours a day, seven days a week, as compared to traditional banks which usually have quite strict working hours (predominantly Monday to Friday from 9 a.m. to 5 p.m.).

- Speed: The second advantage is transaction speed. Transactions using blockchain can be executed 24/7 and only require processing to be completed in 15 minutes. In contrast, processing transactions is not possible at commercial banks during weekends and bank holidays. Bank transactions can also take much longer to execute, with international wire transfers sometimes taking longer than 24 hours. To conduct such transactions in a traditional bank, the customer needs a bank account, government-issued identification, and a mobile phone as the smallest requirement. However, with blockchain-based transactions, only an internet connection and mobile phone are needed. With the emergence of digital banking applications, traditional banks' customers are now only as safe as their online application server.
- Security: Third, the security of blockchain-based cryptocurrencies increases with the growth of its network. Furthermore, as the cryptocurrency system is still relatively young and not very widely adopted, it is recommended that cryptocurrencies are stored in cold storage where they are inaccessible to hackers.

Drawbacks

- Cost: One of the main disadvantages of blockchain-based technologies is their high technical costs for mining the currencies, which can result in high technology and electricity expenses relative to their output. In this case, printing fiat money may be a cheaper method.
- Size: Another difficulty with blockchain-enabled cryptocurrencies is their small size, which can lead to a shortage of transactions.
- Lack of regulations: Additionally, a potential problem with blockchain technology is the current lack of regulation, which limits the participation of larger institutional investors. The lack of regulation can also result in abuse of the users' right to privacy, which has recently led to the exploitation of blockchain-based technologies for illegal purposes.

Chapter Summary

- The financial services sector is about to undergo a significant shift as a result of the emergence of blockchain and other disruptive technologies.
- There was a rapid growth of newly developed start-ups that saw the potential of using digitalization in combination with traditional banks' business models to offer new digital products and services for the financial sector.
- FinTech users can be divided into the following categories:
- business-to-business (B2B) for banks: This category refers to FinTech products and services that are intended for use by banks themselves, rather than by individual consumers or small businesses. The United Kingdom, Singapore, China,

India, and Canada have created regulatory sandboxes and published guidelines for a variety of FinTech applications, including mobile banking, digital payments, and digital and online banking.

- Smart contracts are a promising innovation enabled by blockchain technology that can streamline the process of conducting business and legal agreements, increase trust and security, and reduce costs.
- Distributed applications can eliminate or reduce the need for intermediaries in transactions and give customers access to peer-to-peer lending and cryptocurrencies.
- Security tokens will lead to less expensive and quicker first security offerings and will also set up automated and more standardized processes in terms of regulations.
- Distributive ledger is a technology that enables users to store and retrieve data by a certain set of assets and their holders in a shared database.
- Blockchain-enabled cryptocurrencies are small in size, which can lead to a shortage of transactions.

Discussion Questions
- How is FinTech changing the traditional banking and financial services industry?
- What are the potential benefits and drawbacks of using blockchain technology in finance?
- How do smart contracts work and what industries can receive help from their use?
- How does a distributed ledger differ from a traditional centralized ledger system?
- What are some current real-world applications of blockchain technology?
- How does the use of blockchain technology impact security and privacy in the financial industry?
- What are some of the regulatory challenges facing the implementation of blockchain and FinTech?
- How do you think the use of blockchain and FinTech will evolve in the next 5–10 years?
- How do you think blockchain technology will affect the way we think about trust and transparency in financial transactions?
- What are some of the most exciting or innovative projects currently using blockchain technology in finance?

Learn from the Web
Khan Academy:
- Blockchain and Bitcoin course (www.khanacademy.org/economics-finance-domain/core-finance/money-and-banking/bitcoin/v/bitcoin-what-is-it)
- Distributed ledger technology course (www.khanacademy.org/economics-finance-domain/core-finance/money-and-banking)

Coursera:
- Smart contracts course (gb.coursera.org/learn/smarter-contracts)
- Introduction to FinTech course (gb.coursera.org/courses?query=fintech)

Udemy:
- Blockchain and Bitcoin fundamentals course (www.udemy.com/topic/Blockchain/)
- Smart contracts and solidity course (www.udemy.com/topic/smart-contracts/)

References

Benos, E., Garratt, R., & Gurrola-Perez, P. (2017). The economics of distributed ledger technology for securities settlement. *Available at SSRN 3023779*.

Blockchain.com (2023). Blockchain size. [Online] Available at: https://www.Blockchain.com/explorer/charts/blocks-size

Blandin, A., Pieters, G. C., Wu, Y., Dek, A., Eisermann, T., Njoki, D., & Taylor, S. (2020). 3rd global cryptoasset benchmarking study. *Available at SSRN 3700822*.

CB Insights (2022). State of Fintech. [Online] Available at: https://www.cbinsights.com/reports/CB-Insights_Fintech-Report-Q2-2022.pdf

CoinGecko (2023). Ethereum Price Chart (ETH). [Online] Available at: https://www.coingecko.com/en/coins/ethereum#panel

Deloitte (2020). Are token assets the securities of tomorrow? Avaiable at: https://www2.deloitte.com/content/dam/Deloitte/lu/Documents/technology/lu-token-assets-securities-tomorrow.pdf

Estevez, E. (2020). What Is Open Banking? [Online] Available at: https://www.investopedia.com/terms/o/open-banking.asp

EYGM Limited (2019). Global FinTech Adoption Index 2019. Avaiable at: https://assets.ey.com/content/dam/ey-sites/ey-com/en_gl/topics/banking-and-capital-markets/ey-global-fintech-adoption-index.pdf

Glaser, F., & Bezzenberger, L. (2015, March). Beyond cryptocurrencies-a taxonomy of decentralized consensus systems. In *23rd European conference on information systems (ECIS), Münster, Germany*.

Glaser, F. (2017). Pervasive Decentralisation of Digital Infrastructures: A Framework for Blockchain enabled System and Use Case Analysis. [Online] Available at: https://pdfs.semanticscholar.org/859d/0535e16095f274df4d69df54954b21258a13.pdf

Gopie, N. (2018). What are smart contracts on blockchain? [Online] Available at: https://www.ibm.com/blogs/Blockchain/2018/07/what-are-smart-contracts-on-Blockchain/

Gradstein, H. L., Krause, S. K. & Natarajan, H. (2017). Distributed Ledger Technology (DLT) and Blockchain; *FinTech Note No. 1*, Washington DC: International Bank for Reconstruction and Development/The World Bank.

Gupta, P. & Tham, T. M. (2018). *FinTech: The New DNA of Financial Services: The New DNA of Financial Services*. Boston, Germany: DEG Press.

Juniper Research (2021). Number of open banking users worldwide in 2020 with forecasts from 2021 to 2024, by region (in millions) [Graph]. In Statista. [Online] Available at: https://www.statista.com/statistics/1228771/open-banking-users-worldwide/?locale=en

Levi, S. D. & Lipton, A. B. (2018). An Introduction to Smart Contracts and their Potential and Inherent Limitations, s.l.: Harvard Law School.

Liskov, B. & Castro, M. (2002). Practical Byzantine Fault Tolerance and Proactive Recovery. In: s.l.:s.n., pp. 398–461.

Majaski, C. (2020). Cryptocurrency Security Token: Definition, Forms, Investing In. [Online] Available at: https://www.investopedia.com/terms/s/security-token.asp

Nakamoto, S. (2008). Bitcoin: A Peer-to-Peer Electronic Cash System. [Online] Available at: https://bitcoin.org/bitcoin.pdf

Open Banking Europe (2021). Building a Digital Europe. [Online] Available at: https://www.openbanking.exchange/europe

Pinna, A. & Ruttenberg, W. (2016). Distributed ledger technologies in securities post-trading. s.l.: European Central Bank.

Platt, C. (2017). Thoughts on the taxonomy of blockchains & distributed ledger technologies. [Online] Available at: https://medium.com/@colin_/thoughts-on-the-taxonomy-of-Blockchains-distributed-ledger-technologies-ecad1c819e28

PwC (2021). Venture Capital Funding Report Q4 2020. Available at: https://www.cbinsights.com/research/report/venture-capital-q4-2020/

Rauchs, M., Glidden, A., Gordon, B., Pieters, G. C., Recanatini, M., Rostand, F., Vagneur, K. & Zhang, B. Z. (2018). Distributed ledger technology systems: A conceptual framework. Available at SSRN 3230013.

Settipalli, L., Gangadharan, G. R., & Bellamkonda, S. (2023). An extended lightweight Blockchain based collaborative healthcare system for fraud prevention. *Cluster Computing*, 1–11.

Sokolin, L. (2019). The Future of FinTech. [Online] Available at: https://www.investopedia.com/the-future-of-FinTech-4770491

Tasca, P. & Tessone, C. (2018). Taxonomy of Blockchain Technologies. Principles of Identification and Classification. [Online] Available at: https://papers.ssrn.com/sol3/papers.cfm?abstract_id=2977811

World Economic Forum. (2016). The future of financial infrastructure. Available at: https://www3.weforum.org/docs/WEF_The_future_of_financial_infrastructure.pdf

Further Reading

Nakamoto, S. (2008). Bitcoin: A Peer-to-Peer Electronic Cash System. [Online] Available at: https://bitcoin.org/bitcoin.pdf

Gupta, P. and Tham, T. M. (2018). Fintech: The New DNA of Financial Services. DEG Press.

Glaser, F. (2017). Pervasive Decentralisation of Digital Infrastructures: A Framework for Blockchain enabled System and Use Case Analysis. [Online] Available at: https://pdfs.semanticscholar.org/859d/0535e16095f274df4d69df54954b21258a13.pdf

2 Evolution of Cryptocurrency and Digital Currencies

Introduction

Cryptocurrency is not backed by a single entity; rather, its user base provides the currency with its purchasing power. Technically speaking, it is a type of code generated through the "mining" process that is tracked and maintained by the blockchain – a digital ledger that guarantees transparency throughout the entire process. A cryptocurrency is a digital or virtual currency that is protected by cryptography, making it very hard to counterfeit or spend twice (Frankenfield, 2020). Blockchain technology, which is a distributed ledger maintained by a network of computers, is the foundation of many cryptocurrencies.

The usage of cryptocurrencies as a means of electronic payment has become one of its most famous applications in recent years. For instance, in 2019, Facebook unveiled Libra, its own cryptocurrency that aimed to simplify the process of sending money to others via smartphones. Additionally, a lot of companies have started using Bitcoin as payment for their goods and services, including Microsoft, AT&T, and Overstock.

Central banks launching their own digital currency is another illustration. The Monetary Authority of Singapore and the Bank of Canada have already started experimenting with their own central bank digital currencies (CBDCs), while the European Central Bank has declared ambitions to introduce a digital euro soon.

Features of Cryptocurrency

Another characteristic of cryptocurrencies that significantly sets them apart from conventional fiat currencies is ownership. The majority of cryptocurrencies are privately issued and have no connection to any kind of central or governmental body. Since they are largely uncontrolled, this also holds true for their regulation. However, given

https://doi.org/10.1515/9783110982398-002

that certain agencies have already started to implement or pass legislation for cryptocurrencies, this approach to regulation may alter soon.

The first cryptocurrency, Bitcoin, was made available as open-source software. After its release, others were made as a result. Online communities employ cryptocurrencies as tokens because they are powered by algorithms and are supported by certain technologies. However, they are now being used to pay for physical products and services. They are frequently used for peer-to-peer payments. Since they are based on cryptography, they are regarded as secure and dependable.

The digital equivalent of traditional fiat cash is known as digital currency. It is transportable and withdrawable from ATMs. It is a balance or record that is typically kept in an online distributed database. Another type of digital currency is cryptocurrency. Although they are not physically present, digital currencies share many of the same traits as other forms of money. They permit instantaneous transactions because of this. While they do not originate from central banks, they do offer a digital representation of wealth. They can, however, be used in place of cash. In other words, they are another name for the currency that is used to pay for products and services electronically. Figure 2.1 presents the features of cryptocurrency, which include:

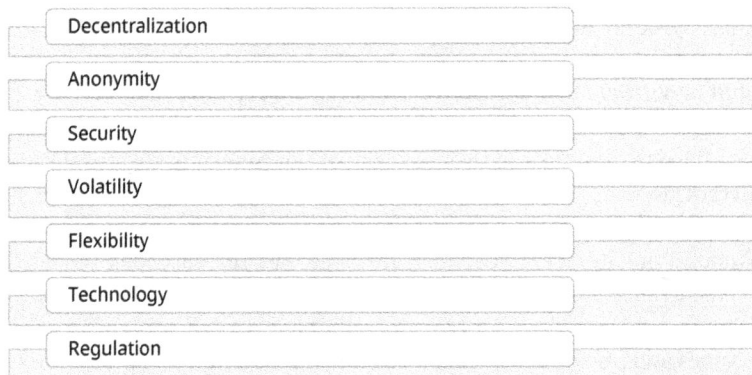

| Decentralization |
| Anonymity |
| Security |
| Volatility |
| Flexibility |
| Technology |
| Regulation |

Figure 2.1: Features of cryptocurrency.

- Decentralization: Cryptocurrency is created through a process known as mining and is not backed by a single entity. On a blockchain, a widely used public digital ledger, transactions are verified and recorded.
- Anonymity: Transactions involving cryptocurrencies are anonymous; therefore, the identity of the party initiating the transaction is kept a secret.
- Security: Cryptography protects cryptocurrencies, making it very hard to forge or double-spend them.
- Volatility: The price of a cryptocurrency can change drastically and quickly.

- Flexibility: Cryptocurrency is a type of digital asset rather than actual money because it only exists digitally and can be kept in a digital wallet.
- Blockchain technology: To ensure transparency and security, cryptocurrency transactions are recorded on a distributed ledger known as the blockchain.
- Regulating cryptocurrency: Although it is still mostly unregulated, certain nations have started to do so.

Differences Between Cryptocurrencies and Digital Currencies

Digital currency and cryptocurrencies can be isolated with the following differences:
- Centralization: The ability to control transactions is the primary distinction between digital currency and cryptocurrencies. While cryptocurrencies are mostly autonomous and unregulated, digital currencies require a centralized network for monitoring. Some cryptocurrencies, nevertheless, are completely centralized and run by institutions.
- Performance: Cryptocurrency outperforms digital currency in terms of cryptography. Cryptocurrencies are recorded on a blockchain and the coins are held in "wallets" that offer a better level of cybersecurity, whereas digital currencies do not need any particular native ways to be encrypted.
- Transparency: Cryptocurrencies are transparent, whereas digital currencies are not. In the case of digital currencies, it is impossible to choose a wallet's address, and the data is kept private and discreet. With cryptocurrencies, all transactions and revenue sources are visible to the user. Information about Bitcoin transactions is available to the public and is kept on a decentralized ledger. Because of this, digital currency transactions require administrative challenges while cryptocurrency transactions may readily be tracked in the event of a dispute.
- Stability: The global financial market more widely accepts digital currency as they are stable. The bulk of people can understand it and exchange it. However, cryptocurrency is still a niche market that needs to build trust.
- Legality: Since cryptocurrencies operate outside of established legal frameworks and are not backed by any government, their legality is a hotly contested topic in many nations. However, debates concerning their legality have been prompted by their use and market position.

History and Development of Cryptocurrencies

Through a nine-page white paper by Nakamoto (2008), titled *Bitcoin: A Peer-to-Peer Electronic Cash System*, Bitcoin became well known. Twelve chapters that each elaborate on a different topic related to the recently created cryptocurrency make up Nakamoto's paper.

Due to the fact that banks and other financial institutions are unable to avoid resolving conflicts, Nakamoto underlines the significance of non-reversible transactions,
which are not achievable in the existing financial system. This is referred to as the
trust-based model challenge. Due to the necessity to adjudicate disagreements, which
incurs additional expenses and renders microtransactions impossible, such a model
typically has higher transaction costs. Nakamoto draws a comparison between the
current system of transactions and an electronic payment system.

But how and on what basis do these transactions operate? Bitcoin transactions are
described as an "electronic coin as a sequence of digital signatures" (Nakamoto, 2008).
The concept underlying these exchanges is that the owner of a coin adds it to a chain of
coins that have already been transferred by other coin owners. This is accomplished by
digitally signing a hash of an earlier transaction and making the digital public key available for use by other participants in the chain. Nakamoto chose not to utilize an intermediary (bank or financial institution) in order to prevent the issue of double-spending
and instead concentrated on the significance of the earliest transaction, which is the
one that counts and further attempts to double-spend are not taken into consideration.

The prior timestamp was added to make sure that even if a transaction were deleted without the consent of all other chain participants, its timestamp would still be
observable and traceable. Nakamoto developed a proof-of-work method similar to
Adam Back's hashcash to enable the timestamp server to be used on a peer-to-peer concept. The method finds a value that provides the block's hash with the necessary zero
bits by increasing a nonce in the block. The block and the data it contains cannot be
modified once the operation is finished. The block is added following a particular transaction (Nakamoto, 2008). Only when every newly added transaction has been changed
are changes permitted.

With the inclusion of the previous timestamp, it was ensured that even if someone
found a way to delete a transaction without the consensus of all other participants in
the chain, its timestamp would still be visible and trackable. To make the timestamp
server usable on a peer-to-peer concept, Nakamoto came up with a proof-of-work system like Adam Back's hashcash. The system works by incrementing a nonce in the
block until a value is found that gives the block's hash the required zero bits. Once the
process is completed, the block and the data it holds cannot be changed anymore. The
block is added after a specific transaction. Changes are only possible if all newly added
transactions are altered (Nakamoto, 2008).

Proof of work also solves the problem of fraudulent majority decision-making as
it only allows one vote per central processing unit (CPU) rather than one vote per IP
address that can be manipulated. Therefore, if an attacker wanted to alter a specific
block, they would need to alter the proof of work of the block they want to access,
and the proofs of work of all blocks added to the chain after it. Nakamoto proposes
simplified payment verification.

Therefore, the user would be unable to check their transactions themselves. However, they can link the transaction to a place on the blockchain, and from there observe

whether the network node has accepted the transaction. Additional confirmations are the blocks added after the transaction. Nakamoto believes that verification is more reliable the longer the chain is. However, it can be more vulnerable in the case of a short chain, as the attacker would find it easier to obtain majority power over the network or chain. In this case, Nakamoto states the protective strategy would be to get automatic alerts from individual block's nodes when they detect a suspicious or invalid block. The software would then download the whole block, including suspicious nodes, and confirm potential inconsistencies.

Privacy is also addressed in the Bitcoin white paper by Nakamoto, as the study indicates that the traditional system of limiting access to information only to the parties involved and trusted third parties can be simplified. Nakamoto believes that public digital keys should be kept anonymous. Therefore, transactions would be visible to the public without any information about the sender or recipient. To improve privacy even further, a new private key should be used for every transaction, preventing transactions from relating to a joint owner. Nakamoto (2008) acknowledges that some linking in multi-input transactions would still be possible even with private keys. Table 2.1 presents key events regarding cryptocurrency.

Table 2.1: Key events regarding cryptocurrency.

Year	Events
2008	A white paper titled *Bitcoin: A Peer-to-Peer Electronic Cash System*, written under the alias Satoshi Nakamoto, introduces the idea of a decentralized digital currency.
	The first Bitcoins are created in January 2009, and Nakamoto and Hal Finney carry out the first Bitcoin transaction.
2010	BitcoinMarket.com, the first Bitcoin exchange, becomes live.
2011	Alternative cryptocurrencies known as "altcoins," such as Litecoin, Ripple, and Namecoin, are first created.
	The Bitcoin Savings and Trust Ponzi scheme raises awareness of the possibility of fraud and scams inside the Bitcoin ecosystem.
2013	This year marks the first year that a single Bitcoin is worth more than $1,000.
	Initial coin offerings (ICOs) start to take off in 2013.
2017	Nearly $20,000 is the all-time high for the price of Bitcoin.
2017	According to a report by the US Securities and Exchange Commission (SEC), some ICOs may qualify as securities and fall under the jurisdiction of federal securities laws.
2018	Creation and launch of the Kryll.io ICO.
2020	The town of Zug in Switzerland allows the opportunity to pay taxes in cryptocurrency.
2021	El Salvador legalizes Bitcoin.

Table 2.1 (continued)

Year	Events
2022	The Ronin network was subject to hack by North Korean state-backed hacking collective, Lazarus Group. Hackers stole around US$625 million worth of Ethereum and the USDC stablecoin.
	FTX and its 30-year-old founder Sam Bankman-Fried went from industry leaders to bankruptcy in a matter of days.
2023	Strict regulations for cryptocurrency trade amid the fall of FTX are implemented

Cryptocurrencies in the World

Thousands of cryptocurrencies are available, and many are now obsolete. According to CoinMarketCap (2023), there were 13,669 cryptocurrencies as of late 2021. Additionally, many tokens are entering the market regularly as it is very easy to create new ones. The Ethereum blockchain facilitates users in launching new tokens by providing its network, so developers can use already available infrastructure instead of building from scratch. Cryptocurrency is popular due to the following three characteristics:
- Utility: The use of cryptocurrency and blockchain technology is rapidly increasing as time passes. The financial industry is evolving constantly, and retailers and service providers widely accept cryptocurrency payments.
- Attractive investment: Cryptocurrency has evolved as one of the most attractive investments worldwide. Its value as an asset class has risen steeply over the last five years and is one of the most debated topics in the financial market. Many people view it as an attractive asset class due to its enormous returns.
- Futurism: It is also widely believed that cryptocurrency is the future of money. Moreover, many businesses throughout the world are exploring ways to use blockchain technology to improve their operations.

Table 2.2 provides a list of the top 10 cryptocurrencies. The value of these currencies changes rapidly, as is the case with most traded companies in the world. However, despite the volatility, a few consistencies can be observed. Bitcoin is at the top, as it has the strongest adoption rate and the largest network of miners. Ethereum's Ether is the second largest, as it also serves as a platform for other users to create new tokens. Many of the cryptocurrencies (listed in the table) rely on the decentralized applications provided by Ethereum.

It is worth noting that there are also risks associated with investing in cryptocurrencies. According to the Federal Trade Commission (FTC) (2022), more than 46,000 people have claimed that they lost over one billion US dollars in crypto to scams since the start of 2021. These losses were 60 times higher than the losses of 2018, with an average individual loss of $2,600. The FTC also reported that, out of these scams, 70% of people

Table 2.2: Ten largest cryptocurrencies in the world.

Rank	Coin Name	Market Cap (in billion GBP)
1	Bitcoin (BTC)	363.1
2	Ethereum (ETH)	159
3	Tether (USDT)	54.8
4	Binance Coin (BNB)	40.0
5	US Dollar Coin (USDC)	34.2
6	XRP (XRP)	16.7
7	Binance USD (BUSD)	13
8	Cardano (ADA)	10.86
9	Dogecoin (DOGE)	9.8
10	Polygon (MATIC)	7.9

Note: *This data is valid as of February 2023.*
Source: coinmarketcap (2023).

made payments in Bitcoin, 10% in Tether, and 9% in Ether. One feature of cryptocurrencies like Bitcoin is that payments cannot be reversed, unlike chargebacks, which allow consumers to reverse a transaction if they claim to have been charged for goods or services they did not receive or were fraudulently charged. These scams often occur on social media platforms; half of the crypto fraud victims reported that they received messages from different social media platforms (e.g., Instagram 32%, Facebook 26%, WhatsApp 9%, and Telegram 7%, as reported by the Federal Trade Commission).

Fraud in Cryptocurrencies

Increasing rates of fraud in the crypto market are due to its features that attract scammers. There is no centralized authority or bank to monitor transactions and prevent fraud. Many individuals involved in crypto are not fully aware of the procedures, making them vulnerable to scammers through social media platforms. Investment scams are among the most common, with reported losses of 575 million US dollars according to the Federal Trade Commission (2022). Scammers typically claim to offer quick and high returns on investments through social media platforms, targeting those with limited knowledge and experience. They may also perform initial withdrawals to gain the trust of investors.

Business and government impersonation scams are the second highest, with 133 million US dollars in reported losses since 2021. These scams often involve text messages about supposedly unauthorized online purchases or fake security alerts from Microsoft. They put a large number of people at risk. Another tactic used by scammers is to impersonate border control agents and claim to be investigating drug trafficking, suggesting that individuals transfer their funds to crypto ATMs as a way to protect their money. In this way, the scammers obtain the individual's QR code and transfer the funds to their own wallet.

Fraud using cryptocurrencies has the potential to seriously harm both people and the industry as a whole. Financial loss for fraud victims is one of the main effects, as con artists may steal money through phishing schemes, Ponzi schemes, and other fraudulent actions. As there may be little to no remedy for people to retrieve stolen funds, these losses could be considerable.

Fraud has a severe effect on the reputation and confidence of the larger cryptocurrency industry. Fraud can create suspicion and mistrust of the market's validity as it grows more widespread. This may deter prospective buyers and users, preventing the growth and widespread use of cryptocurrencies. A few crypto fraud cases are listed below:

– The OneCoin Ponzi scheme: OneCoin was a multi-billion-dollar fraud that made the claim to be a cryptocurrency. It was later discovered to be a fraudulent scam where investors were given returns that were never actually received. The company's founders were detained in 2019 and accused of fraud, money laundering, and other offences.
– The Bitconnect Ponzi scheme: Bitconnect was a platform for lending that offered investors significant profits. But as it turned out to be a Ponzi scheme, the Bitconnect token's value plummeted, costing investors millions of dollars.
– The scam with PlusToken: PlusToken was a platform for investing in cryptocurrencies that offered investors large returns. But it turned out to be a fraud, and the creators were detained in 2019.
– The Bitfinex and Tether scandal: Tether, a stablecoin linked to the US dollar, and Bitfinex, a significant cryptocurrency exchange, were accused of using Tether's reserves to conceal an $850 million loss. There is still debate on whether or not there was an actual fraud in this instance.
– The QuadrigaCX scandal: In 2019, after the death of its founder Gerald Cotten and the discovery that he had sole control over the exchange's funds and had kept them in a cold wallet that he carried to his grave, QuadrigaCX, a Canadian cryptocurrency exchange, collapsed.

Underlying Technologies

As described in Chapter 1, there are two technologies that the majority of cryptocurrencies have in common – those being DLT (distributed ledger technology) and blockchain. While DLT has existed for many decades, blockchain was specifically developed based on DLT to support the successful implementation of Bitcoin and other cryptocurrencies. Blockchain allows for the collection of data from transactions and the addition of a timestamp to each one. Transactions are then grouped into blocks, which are permanently linked in a chain and cannot be altered in any way.

Although blockchain is often the only underlying technology mentioned in relation to cryptocurrencies, it is not the only one. Some cryptocurrencies, while similar to Bitcoin in their use of blockchain, may also use other underlying technologies. However, to ensure secure, anonymous, and direct transactions between two parties, they must always use blockchain. Blockchain technology, often known as decentralized digital ledgers, is the foundation of cryptocurrency. Some of the key characteristics of blockchain are as follows:

–   A blockchain is a type of digital ledger that securely and openly logs all network transactions. Each block in the chain is connected to the one before it and the one after it and records a number of transactions.
–   The blockchain is safe and impenetrable once a block is added to the chain because the data it contains cannot be changed.
–   A blockchain's decentralized nature is one of its key characteristics. A blockchain network is maintained by a network of computers, or nodes, that collaborate to validate and record transactions rather than depending on a central authority.
–   Another crucial aspect of cryptocurrency technology is cryptography, which is used to protect financial transactions and user identities. In cryptography, information is encrypted and decoded using mathematical methods. It is used in the context of cryptocurrencies to safeguard the private keys needed to access and transfer funds.
–   Various consensus methods are also used to approve transactions and register them on the blockchain. Proof of work (PoW) and proof of stake (PoS) are the two techniques that are most frequently used. Users who participate in PoW, also known as mining, compete to validate transactions and resolve mathematical puzzles. In PoS, a more energy-efficient method, the users who hold the most cryptocurrency are selected to validate transactions. Overall, the underlying technologies in cryptocurrency include decentralized digital ledgers (blockchain), cryptography, and consensus mechanism. These technologies make it possible for users to securely and transparently transfer and store value without the need for a central authority.

Frameworks of Crypto and Digital Currencies

As the framework of Bitcoin has already been discussed in detail, this section will focus on some of the other better-known cryptocurrencies that use similar, as well as completely different, frameworks compared to Bitcoin. We will observe the frameworks of Ethereum and Ripple. While Ripple is in some ways similar to Bitcoin, it focuses more on digital payment protocols.

Ethereum

Ethereum, compared to Bitcoin, uses a different approach and is used for different purposes. Ethereum was launched in 2015. Ethereum is open access to digital money and data-friendly services for everyone – no matter your background or location. It's a community-built technology behind the cryptocurrency ether (ETH) and thousands of applications you can use today.

A significant distinction between Bitcoin and other cryptocurrencies can be seen, even in the most basic definition of Ethereum offered by its creators. Ethereum is programmable and allows its users and developers to do much more than just use it as a cryptocurrency, even though it is based on the same principles as Bitcoin and has its own crypto coin. Ethereum offers a marketplace of different financial services, such as smart contracts, games, and applications (distributed applications) that protect consumers' data and identity. Overall, Ethereum builds on the same platform that Bitcoin has established. However, the development of a wide range of open-source services that can be made feasible through blockchain expands the use of blockchain even further.

Ripple

Ripple is the third-largest cryptocurrency by market capitalization, after Bitcoin and Ethereum, with a market capitalization of around 22 billion USD in early 2021, according to the CoinMarketCap (2021) website. Ripple is similar to Bitcoin in many ways. It operates via blockchain, and its currency is called XRP. However, there are again some aspects that Ripple does differently. Ripple focuses mainly on digital payment protocols, better known as the cryptocurrency XRP. According to Frankenfield (2019), it operates like other crypto platforms as a peer-to-peer, open-source, decentralized platform that simplifies and makes money transfers as seamless as possible. This is meant for any type of currency, such as EUR, USD, Bitcoin, or XRP, just to give a few examples.

Ripple does not operate via proof-of-work or proof-of-stake systems, while being comparable to other cryptocurrencies in many aspects. Instead, it uses a system where transactions rely on a consensus protocol between two parties. Frankenfield explains the consensus system as an improvement of the systems' integrity and prevention of double-spending, which was also the primary goal when establishing Bitcoin. Multiple gateways are used when a transaction is started using the Ripple system.

However, when the money is sent to the gateway systems, all but the first transactions are deleted. To determine which transaction has been done first and which to delete, a poll is conducted between the distributed nodes, and consensus is reached by a majority vote. Therefore, confirmations can be almost instant and take up to five seconds. According to Frankenfield, similarly to Bitcoin and Ethereum, there is no central authority that oversees reaching a consensus and wiring the transaction. The Ripple platform is known as decentralized.

Ripple is currently available across more than 55 countries and can trade in more than 120 currencies. It also takes advantage of its own cryptocurrency, XRP, which is the base of its transactions, as Ripple has set fixed minimum transaction costs at 0.00001 XRP, which in early 2021 calculates to 0.00000425 EUR. This makes transactions much cheaper compared to traditional banks. Another great advantage compared to present fiat currencies is, according to Frankenfield, transaction times. Even with the high frequency of transactions on the Ripple network, transfers are usually settled in a couple of seconds. Compared to traditional banks, that could take days, if not even a week, to process and complete a cross-border wire transfer. That makes Ripple's digital payment protocol much more desirable to customers who deal with a more significant number of cross-border transfers.

Price Stability

When talking about the potential of CBDCs and what can be learned from cryptocurrencies, the stability of their pricing is a crucial factor to take into account. Figure 2.2 outlines the price of Bitcoin and highlights this volatility over the currency's history through changes in both price and transaction volume.

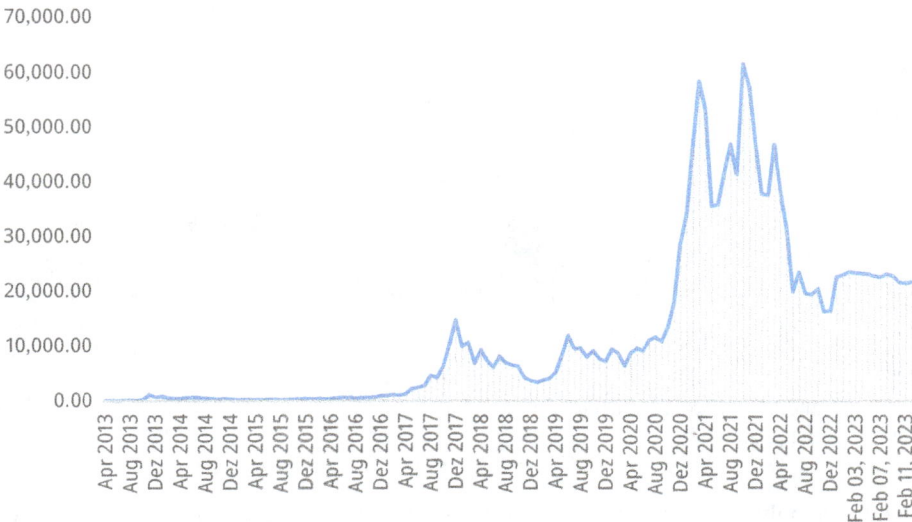

Figure 2.2: Bitcoin's price volatility.
Source: CoinGecko.com (2023)

Figure 2.2 illustrates how the price of Bitcoin has become increasingly volatile, despite the absence of any underlying factors that might cause significant increases or decreases in value. In 2017, a rapid growth occurred when Bitcoin reached as high as 19,000 USD. Without any apparent reason, its value dropped to around 7,000 USD in the following months and even dropped to around 3,500 USD in 2018. At the beginning of 2021, the price of Bitcoin was once again bullish, reaching just below 40,000 USD. Interestingly, despite the world being at a standstill due to the COVID-19 pandemic in 2020, the price of Bitcoin continued to grow. These two instances demonstrate that Bitcoin's growth is not highly correlated with global market conditions.

In addition to price volatility, the volume of transactions also exhibits a similar pattern, as presented in Figure 2.3. The fact that cryptocurrencies are only available in digital form and are not backed by tangible assets creates another problem. The price of Bitcoin is directly connected to the increasing amount of energy needed to obtain them. Therefore, energy prices might be a potential threat to the stability of Bitcoin, primarily due to the ever-increasing need for electricity. Substantial price increases could occur in the future, which could put the stability of Bitcoin and other cryptocurrencies at risk.

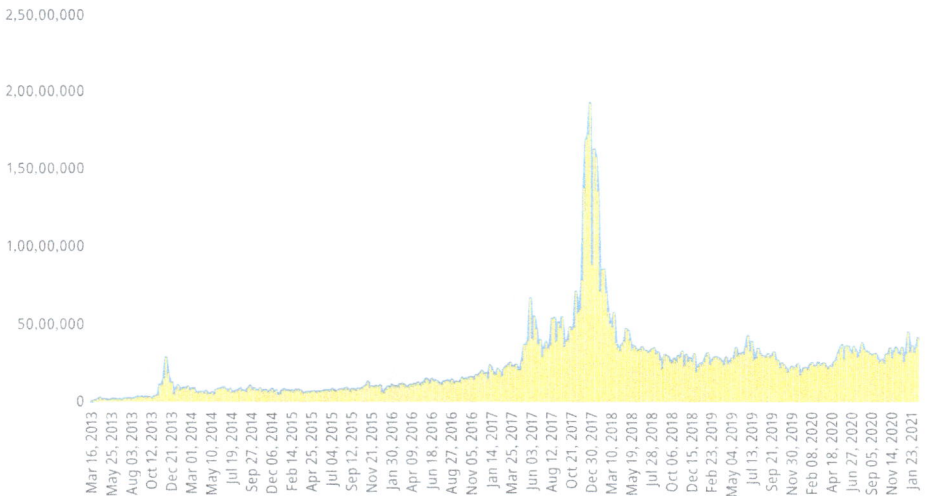

Figure 2.3: Bitcoin's transaction volume.
Source: Statista (2022)

The digital-only nature of cryptocurrencies is another potential risk to their stability. Despite the use of private and public keys and various proofs, cryptocurrencies are not immune to cyberattacks. In May 2019, the largest single theft of Bitcoin occurred, as reported by the BBC (2019) and other major media outlets. The Binance exchange, which stores and transfers significant amounts of Bitcoins and other cryptocurrencies for its customers, was the target of the cyberattack. It was reported that hackers had stolen 7,000 Bitcoins in a single attack, which would have been worth around 41 million USD at the time and would be worth 280 million USD at the peak price of Bitcoin in 2021. This event highlights the vulnerability of cryptocurrencies, as large amounts can be stolen at once and never found again.

It is important to note that cryptocurrencies are not completely safe; there are many potential threats that could destabilize cryptocurrency markets. The size of cryptocurrency markets and their independent currencies is one of the problems. When compared to fiat currencies that are backed by governments, the majority of cryptocurrencies have small market capitalizations and can destabilize much more quickly.

Regulation of Cryptocurrencies

As the importance of crypto-assets has grown over time, discussions about how to handle and regulate them have become more prevalent. Different nations have adopted various strategies, with regulations ranging from restrictive to supportive.

Regulation in Europe

The Token and TT Service Provider Act (TVTG), also known as the Blockchain Act, was enacted by Liechtenstein on October 3, 2019, making it the first country in Europe to implement national regulation. The law entered into force on January 1, 2020. The main concern of the supervisory aspect of the law is to define when trusted technology service providers will be supervised and how they will be registered. The civil law aspect deals with more complex topics, such as token definition, rights of ownership and disposal of tokens, and related legal matters.

The government of Liechtenstein does not intend to restrict the advancement of blockchain technologies, but rather seeks to foster it and direct its growth in a legitimate and fraud-free direction. The law was established to protect users and ensure confidence in digital legal transactions, and to describe the rights and obligations of service providers who perform activities on trusted technology systems.

The Liechtenstein Blockchain Act is the first national regulation implemented in Europe. The act is divided into two main parts:

– Supervisory aspect: The supervisory part focuses on defining when and how TT service providers will be supervised and registered, while the civil law aspects deal with more complex topics, such as token definition, ownership rights, and disposal of tokens.

– Regulatory aspect: The act is designed to protect users and ensure confidence in digital legal transactions by establishing a new civil law as a foundation for governing possession, ownership, and disposition rights over tokens.

The Liechtenstein Blockchain Act is unique in that it regulates and establishes the legal framework for the tokenization of tangible assets, such as security tokens, in addition to cryptocurrencies. It also streamlines and clarifies the procedure for launching a new FinTech or blockchain business. All new businesses must register as TT service providers. Liechtenstein has taken a supportive approach to the regulation of crypto-assets and there are many aspects that the European Union and other countries could learn from it.

On the European Union level, the European Commission recently released a proposal for a Regulation of the European Parliament and the Council on Markets in Crypto-assets (MiCA), and amending Directive (EU) 2019/1937. MiCA is part of the digital finance package that aims to support the development of crypto-assets and FinTech while maintaining safety for participants and providers. The package also includes a new strategy on digital finance in the EU space, which aims to embrace the digital future and support the growth of the digital sector. The benefits of digital finance will be made available to EU citizens, according to the European Commission, which wants to support creative European businesses.

According to the European Commission (2020), the main objective of MiCA is not to restrict digital development but to support the growth of new technologies. The digital finance package, therefore, represents the first concrete step towards regulation of digital assets in the EU.

The European Commission states that "crypto-assets are one of the major applications of blockchain technology in finance." The Commission has been conducting extensive research on crypto-assets since the FinTech Action Plan was published in March 2018. The first action was taken in December 2017 during a decline in the capitalization of crypto-assets, when the European Commission wrote to the European Banking Authority (EBA) and the European Securities and Markets Authority (ESMA) and requested that they issue warnings to investors.

In the FinTech Action Plan, the EBA and the ESMA were chosen to research and study the applicability and suitability of EU financial services regulations for use in crypto-asset regulations. According to the European Commission (2020), in 2019, the ESMA issued advice that the application of EU legislation may not be as straightforward as previously thought. The Commission, along with the EBA, found that most crypto-assets may fall outside of EU regulations concerning the combating of money laundering and terrorism financing. Such cryptocurrency assets would not be subject to market integrity and investor and consumer protection provisions, which have a significant impact on the escalation of the mentioned risks. MiCA also focuses on a relatively new field of crypto-assets, known as stablecoins.

With MiCA, the European Commission has responded to various regulation issues surrounding crypto-assets. The Commission plans to introduce an EU-wide framework that will not only regulate but also support the development of digital assets, crypto-currencies, and tokenization. It is planned to create broader possibilities for DLT usage in financial services. Along with MiCA, the European Commission also suggests clarifying the term "financial instruments," which defines the scope of the Markets in Financial Instruments Directive II (MiFID II), to achieve this. They propose that MiFID II now includes DLT-based financial instruments.

Regulation in the United States

In the United States, the regulation of crypto-assets is under the oversight of both state and federal governments. Like in Europe, there are various supervisory bodies on the federal level, including the:
– Securities and Exchange Commission (SEC),
– Commodities Futures Trading Commission (CFTC),
– Department of the Treasury,
– Financial Crimes Enforcement Network (FinCEN),
– Federal Trade Commission (FTC), and
– Office of the Comptroller of the Currency (OCC).

Despite a growing interest in regulation in recent years, only a few regulations have been implemented. Many decision-makers have recognized the potential of new technology and the value of promoting it rather than overregulating it, which would drive new technologies and patents outside of the US.

In the United States, the regulation of cryptocurrencies is under the observation of both state and federal governments. Each US state has the right to regulate cryptocurrencies in its own particular manner, resulting in various laws and regulations affecting cryptocurrencies. Two methods are most frequently used today: first, a very benevolent policy that exempts crypto-assets from state securities regulation, with the expectation that this will attract new investments and improve the state's financial position and public services. Dewey (2020) gives the example of Wyoming, where a new type of bank or special purpose depository institutions will be created for crypto-assets, allowing businesses to hold digital assets in a safe and regulated manner. Other states, such as Colorado, Ohio, and Oklahoma, have also introduced laws to support and promote the use of cryptocurrencies.

Second, some states have chosen to prohibit cryptocurrencies altogether. For example, Iowa introduced a bill that prohibits the state from accepting payments with cryptocurrencies, while a further 10 or so states have issued statements cautioning against cryptocurrency investment. The state of New York is in the middle, transitioning to become a more welcoming state for cryptocurrencies.

An interesting aspect of cryptocurrency regulation in the US is their mining. According to Dewey, the regulation of mining is relatively straightforward, with the principle that "if you are able to own and use cryptocurrency where you live, you should also be able to mine cryptocurrency in that location as well. The new crypto framework from the White House has some important lessons that can be learned. These are as follows.

The White House has recently unveiled a new framework for crypto regulation, which includes measures to combat illegal activity in the sector. According to an official fact sheet from the White House (2022), the US President is considering calling upon Congress to amend existing laws, such as the Bank Secrecy Act, anti-tip-off statutes, and laws against unlicensed money transmitting, to apply explicitly to digital asset service providers. This includes digital asset exchanges and non-fungible token (NFT) platforms. Additionally, the President is evaluating the possibility of increasing fines for sending unlicensed money, as well as amending federal laws to enable the Department of Justice to prosecute crimes involving digital assets, wherever a victim is discovered. These measures are intended to address illegal activity in the sector and establish the US as a leader in the governance of the digital assets ecosystem.

The framework also suggests that a digital version of the dollar (a CBDC) issued by the US central bank, could have "significant benefits." Electronic US dollars, which are partially backed by reserves, are currently held in commercial bank accounts across the nation. Additionally, a number of stablecoins, such as Tether and USD Coin, are pegged to the US dollar. The Federal Reserve's version of a CBDC, known as the hypothetical digital dollar, would be a fully regulated and supported version of the American dollar, governed by a central authority.

The Federal Reserve's version of a CBDC could make it possible for a payment system that is "more efficient, provides a foundation for further technological innovation, facilitates faster cross-border transactions, and is environmentally sustainable," according to the White House's new framework. The report also suggests that it could promote financial inclusion and equity by enabling access for a broad set of consumers. The administration has asked the Fed to continue its ongoing analysis, testing, and evaluation of a CBDC. The fact sheet states that the Treasury will complete an assessment on non-fungible tokens by July 2023 and an assessment on illicit finance risk relating to decentralized finance by the end of February 2023.

According to the White House, stablecoins are a particular subset of cryptocurrencies with a value linked to a physical asset, such as a fiat currency, the US dollar, or a commodity like gold. Central bankers and US lawmakers have expressed concerns about the rise of stablecoins, as they have no control over the regulation of this market and are worried about their growing use in both domestic and international transactions.

The collapse of a popular US dollar-pegged stablecoin project, TerraUSD, in 19 May 2022, resulted in a loss of tens of billions of dollars for investors and has been likened to a bank run. This project had gained credibility thanks to widespread support and public service announcements from reputable financial institutions, but ultimately failed. According to the White House, this failure resulted in a string of bankruptcies that destroyed nearly $600 billion in wealth. They also warn that, in the absence of proper regulation, stablecoins may lead to disruptive runs.

To address these concerns, the White House's framework states that the Treasury will collaborate with other agencies to "identify, track, and analyse emerging strategic risks that relate to digital asset markets," as well as "work with financial institutions to bolster their capacity to identify and mitigate cyber vulnerabilities by sharing information and promoting a wide range of data sets and analytical tools."

Regulation in Asia

Between July 2020 and June 2021, cryptocurrency in Asia experienced rapid growth, with Central and South Asian transactions increasing by 706% and totaling $572.5 billion, or 14% of all cryptocurrency transactions worldwide. The region has a history of embracing new technology and the uptake of cryptocurrencies and blockchain confirms this trend. Regulators have had to pay attention as nearly half of all cryptocurrency trades worldwide take place in Asia, primarily due to an increase in businesses providing services related to the cryptocurrency industry.

China's digital yuan is one of the studied CBDCs and their regulations are taken into consideration as part of the research. China is treating the regulation of FinTech very seriously, and according to Gongsheng (2021), they started regulating FinTech as soon as the sector began to develop. They have put in place a prudent but effective and inclusive regulatory environment, initially based on fairness and tolerance. In China, the FinTech sector is led by Alipay and WeChat Pay, which also account for the most significant growth. Recently, China's regulators have focused on closing regulatory gaps and implementing consumer protection measures to prevent non-bank payment institutions from stealing their customers' money.

According to KPMG's 2019 ranking, three Chinese FinTech companies have ranked in the top 10 global FinTech companies. As per KPMG and H2 Ventures' (2019) results, it is clear that FinTech regulation is becoming more favorable in China. In 2020, there was a significant increase in the opening of new international financial services, and the easing of China's FinTech regulations creates a huge opportunity for CBDC development. It is anticipated that China will attempt to further liberalize its FinTech industry in order to welcome more western FinTech firms, which could make it even simpler for them to create their own CBDC. In Asia, the regulatory environment for cryptocurrencies is diverse and constantly evolving. Some countries, such as China, have banned mining of cryptocurrencies due to concerns about energy consumption. Other nations, like North Korea, have used cryptocurrencies to circumvent Western sanctions and finance their nuclear missile program.

The regulatory framework for institutional and retail investors also varies widely. While some nations, such as Myanmar and Bhutan, have recognized stablecoins and are developing CBDCs, others, like Bangladesh, have imposed strict restrictions on cryptocurrency trading. In Singapore and Thailand, the laws tend to be more lenient, but there has been a recent crackdown on licensing, anti-money laundering (AML), and counter terrorist financing (CTF) regulations. In countries like the Philippines and Indonesia, cryptocurrencies are mainly used as a means of sending money, particularly for the unbanked population, but they must still abide by risk analysis, AML, and CFT regulations. Some well-established cryptocurrency businesses, such as Crypto.com and Tether, are based in Asia, particularly in Hong Kong and Singapore.

Regulation in Africa

Cryptocurrency regulation in Africa is a complex and evolving subject. As the continent's economy expands, the regulation of digital currencies is becoming more and more important. Over the past few years, the use of cryptocurrencies has grown substantially on the African continent, with several countries embracing the technology and its potential to totally revolutionize the financial sector. Meanwhile, governments and financial institutions are concerned about the lack of regulation.

To ensure the safety and security of customers, many African countries have begun to establish cryptocurrency laws. The regulations governing consumer protection, the implementation of anti-money laundering measures, and the registration of cryptocurrency exchanges vary from country to country.

Significant Advantages and Disadvantages of Cryptocurrencies

Advantages of Cryptocurrencies

According to Frankenfield (2020), one of the main advantages of cryptocurrencies is the ability to directly transfer funds between two parties without the need for a third-party intermediary, such as a bank or financial institution. The security of these transactions is maintained through the use of public and private keys and consensus systems, such as proof-of-work and proof-of-stake, and these systems also tend to have minimal costs, making microtransactions possible. Additionally, digital wallets, which consist of a public key for receiving funds and a private key for signing transactions, provide another advantage of using cryptocurrencies. Other benefits of cryptocurrencies include:
- Speed: Confirmation of a cryptocurrency transaction can happen in a matter of minutes, whereas traditional financial transfers may take at least a day to clear.

- Lower fees: The cost of using cryptocurrencies is often much lower than that of traditional financial institutions, with free storage and lower international remittance fees.
- No barriers to entry: Unlike traditional finance, using cryptocurrency does not require a valid ID or credit check and can be accessible to the unbanked population.
- Security: Storing cash or making online purchases with a debit card is less secure than using cryptocurrency, as a hacker would need access to the private key to steal funds. Additionally, many cryptocurrency transactions are anonymous.

Disadvantages of Cryptocurrencies

According to Frankenfield (2020), one of the main drawbacks of cryptocurrencies is their semi-anonymous nature, which makes them well suited for illegal activities such as money laundering and tax evasion. However, it should be noted that transparency varies among different cryptocurrencies, with some being more private and harder to trace than others.

They also mention the potential for a "51% attack" on a blockchain network, where a bad actor takes over 51% of a network's computing power and can manipulate consensus. To prevent such attacks, the authors suggest that developers design blockchain systems in a robust way that prevents a single entity from commanding more than 50% of computing power. Another potential downside of cryptocurrencies is their unpredictable volatility, which is a result of their unregulated nature. This unpredictability can make it difficult for professional investment firms to make decisions, which is one of the most significant drawbacks of cryptocurrencies. Some other disadvantages to holding cryptocurrency include:

- Lack of insurance: Funds held in cryptocurrency are not covered by insurance, unlike deposits made in a bank account in the United States, which are usually insured up to $250,000 per account holder in case the bank loses the money. If you or your custodian loses your cryptocurrency, there may be no recourse.
- Lack of dispute resolution: There is no way to dispute or reverse a transaction if you accidentally send too much money or do not receive what you were expecting in return. All blockchain-confirmed transactions are final, and the other party must agree to send the money back for you to regain access to it.
- Risk of losing access to funds: If you lose your private key, you will lose access to your funds. The private key is necessary to sign transactions and add them to the blockchain, so it is important to have multiple copies of it on hand.
- High volatility: Many cryptocurrencies have highly unstable values, making them challenging to use as a means of payment or to invest in. Prices can easily fluctuate by more than 10% on any given day.

Chapter Summary

- Cryptocurrency is a type of code generated through the "mining" process that is tracked and maintained by the blockchain.
- A cryptocurrency is a digital or virtual currency that is protected by cryptography, making it very hard to counterfeit or spend twice.
- Cryptocurrency is another name for the currency that is used to pay for products and services electronically.
- Cryptocurrencies are largely uncontrolled and have no connection to any central or governmental body. They share many of the same traits as other forms of money, except they are not physically present.
- Cryptocurrencies are mostly autonomous and unregulated, whereas digital currencies require a centralized network for monitoring.
- The global financial market accepts digital currency more widely and it is stable, but it still needs to build trust.
- Nakamoto (2008) underlines the significance of non-reversible transactions, which are not achievable in the existing financial system.
- It is widely believed that cryptocurrency is the future of money and could revolutionize the way money is exchanged around the world.
- Scammers are targeting individuals involved in the crypto industry for investment scams. Fraud using cryptocurrencies has the potential to seriously harm both people and the industry as a whole.

Discussion Questions

- What are the primary characteristics and advantages of using cryptocurrencies?
- What are the differences between cryptocurrencies and conventional types of money and payment systems?
- What are the dangers and difficulties of investing in cryptocurrencies?
- What factors can influence cryptocurrency value and how is it determined?
- What laws and regulations apply to cryptocurrencies and how are they viewed by governments and financial regulators, etc.?
- What effects does cryptocurrency use have on security and privacy?
- What possible applications beyond digital currency does the technology that powers cryptocurrencies (such as blockchain) have?
- What effects does cryptocurrency have on the world's financial markets and economy?
- What are some of the most exciting and cutting-edge applications for cryptocurrencies that are currently being developed or deployed?

Learn from the Web

CoinMarketCap can be used to perform educational activities on cryptocurrency. CoinMarketCap is available at coinmarketcap.com. It provides a variety of data on several cryptocurrencies, including market capitalization, price, trading volume, and price history. It also provides a portfolio tracking function where students may build a virtual portfolio and monitor the success of the cryptocurrencies they choose.

Additionally, they can assess how their portfolio has performed in relation to the entire market and various indices.

The platform provides an opportunity to perform the following group activity. You can use the following steps:

– Choose one of the top 100 cryptocurrencies on CoinMarketCap in terms of market capitalization to give each student or group of students.
– Ask each group to conduct research and present on one of the following elements of the cryptocurrency they were given:
    i.   Detailed background information and history
    ii.   Technology and how it functions
    iii. Market performance and trends at the moment
    iv.   Applications in the real world and use scenarios
    v.   Prospects and potential advancements for the future
– Have a class discussion on the current situation and prospects of the Bitcoin market after each group presentation.
– As an add-on, you can ask each group to write a brief report on the cryptocurrency they were given, including their findings and predictions in more depth. Each group can then submit their report to the class before taking questions and starting new conversations.

References

BBC (2019). Binance exchange hackers steal bitcoins worth $41m. [Online] Available at: https://www.bbc.com/news/technology-48199375

Bitstamp (2021). Bitcoin. [Online] Available at: https://www.bitstamp.net/markets/btc/insights/

Coinmarketcap (2023). Today's Cryptocurrency Prices by Market Cap. Available at: https://coinmarketcap.com/

CoinGecko.com (2023). Bitcoin Price Chart (BTC). Available at: https://www.coingecko.com/en/coins/bitcoin#panel

Dewey, J. (2020). Blockchain & Cryptocurrency Regulation 2021. Available at: https://www.acc.com/sites/default/files/resources/upload/GLI-BLCH21_E-Edition.pdf

European Commission (2020). Proposal for a Regulation of the European Parliament and the council on markets in crypto-assets, and amending Directive (EU) 2019/1937, Brussels: European Commission. Available at: https://eur-lex.europa.eu/legal-content/EN/TXT/?uri=CELEX%3A52020PC0593

Federal Trade Commission (2022). Reported crypto scam losses since 2021 top $1 billion, says FTC Data Spotlight. Available at: https://www.ftc.gov/business-guidance/blog/2022/06/reported-crypto-scam-losses-2021-top-1-billion-says-ftc-data-spotlight

Frankenfield, J. (2019). Ripple (Cryptocurrency). [Online] Available at: https://www.investopedia.com/terms/r/ripple-cryptocurrency.asp

Frankenfield, J. (2020). Cold Storage: What It Is, How It Works, Theft Protection. Available at: https://www.investopedia.com/terms/c/cold-storage.asp

Gongsheng, P. (2021). How China is tackling fintech risk and regulation. *Financial Times*. [Online] Available at: https://www.ft.com/content/5209685c-aa8e-4f33-92d0-81f9c7a29b3c

KPMG, H2 Ventures (2019). 2019 FinTech100: Leading Global FinTech innovators, s.l.: s.n.

Nakamoto, S. (2008). Bitcoin: A Peer-to-Peer Electronic Cash System. [Online] Available at: https://bitcoin.org/bitcoin.pdf

Statista (2022). Bitcoin (BTC) 24 hour trade volume from January 1, 2021 to November 15, 2022 (in billion US dollars) [Graph]. [Online] Available at: https://www.statista.com/statistics/1272819/bitcoin-trade-volume/?locale=en

White House (2022). FACT SHEET: White House Releases First-Ever Comprehensive Framework for Responsible Development of Digital Assets. Available at: https://www.whitehouse.gov/briefing-room/statements-releases/2022/09/16/fact-sheet-white-house-releases-first-ever-comprehensive-framework-for-responsible-development-of-digital-assets/

Further Reading

Casey, M., & Vigna, P. (2018). *The Truth Machine: The Blockchain and the Future of Everything*. St. Martin's Press.

Hughes, L., Dwivedi, Y. K., Misra, S. K., Rana, N. P., Raghavan, V., & Akella, V. (2019). Blockchain research, practice and policy: Applications, benefits, limitations, emerging research themes and research agenda. *International Journal of Information Management, 49*, 114–129.

Liu, Y., & Tsyvinski, A. (2021). Risks and Returns of Cryptocurrency. *The Review of Financial Studies, 34*(6), 2689–2727.

Narayanan, A., Bonneau, J., Felten, E., Miller, A., & Goldfeder, S. (2016). *Bitcoin and Cryptocurrency Technologies: A Comprehensive Introduction*. Princeton University Press.

Tapscott, D., & Tapscott, A. (2016). *Blockchain Revolution: How the Technology Behind Bitcoin Is Changing Money, Business, and the World*. Penguin.

3 Evolution of Central Bank Digital Currencies

Key Facts on Central Bank Digital Currencies
– Since 2017, the People's Bank of China (PBOC) has been developing a digital yuan and testing it out in a number of cities.
– A public consultation on the possibility of a digital euro is currently being held by the European Central Bank (ECB).
– The Bank of England (BoE) is also looking into the possibility of a digital pound and has said that it will decide in the coming years whether to move forward with a pilot.
– In order to test the technical and practical aspects of issuing a digital currency, the central bank of Sweden (Sveriges Riksbank) launched an e-krona pilot program in late 2020.

Introduction

Central bank digital currencies (CBDCs) have the potential to become the most prevalent technology in the digital and transactions field, significantly impacting all players in the international financial services sector. A technological breakthrough in both the way money is printed and the infrastructure needed for operations is digital currency.

CBDCs are digital financing facilities that are a direct obligation of a central bank and are denominated in the national unit of account (BIS, 2020). They serve as a medium of exchange, a store of value, and a unit of account and are official tender issued by a central bank in digital form. They are fiat money that is created digitally. Currently, the general public can only hold cash issued by a reserve bank in the form of actual currency notes. Only financial institutions and a limited number of authorized banking institutions are permitted to hold central bank money in the form of "reserves."

CBDCs have the ability to be extensively used among individuals, enterprises, and wholesale banking institutions to store value and process payments more securely in their electronic form. With most economies seeing a decline in the use of cash, CBDCs can help a central bank continue to fulfill its mandate of providing money, preserving financial stability, and ensuring continuous access in a fully digital economy. According to Kiff et al. (2020), CBDCs are established by a central bank as a digital version of government-issued money that appears on the liabilities side of a country's monetary authority's balance sheet.

Overview of Central Bank Digital Currencies

Recent years have seen a surge in interest in CBDCs due to advancements in payments and technologies as well as the impact of COVID-19. Seven out of the top 10 global CBDC projects were conducted in the Asia-Pacific (APAC) region, making it the leader in this

https://doi.org/10.1515/9783110982398-003

field. CBDCs have the ability to create a future of value transfer platform that makes the payment systems of economies, businesses, and households more resilient, innovative, and competitive as a result of the increasing globalization and digitalization of financial services. CBDCs can improve the efficiency and effectiveness of a jurisdiction's payment system by providing secure digital currencies to users. In contrast to other less secure digital instruments, CBDCs:

- offer a more reliable option for payments,
- provide a stable store of value, and
- do not threaten monetary and financial stability.

As cash usage decreases and new "value transfer alternatives" are increasingly used in the payment cycle, CBDCs will become even more crucial in the future (Deloitte, 2021). Banking institutions and other financial services providers must prepare for this inevitable change and plan for how it will affect their balance sheets, technologies, and profits.

The growth of CBDCs began to take shape in recent years, with a significant increase after 2017 when China began creating the digital yuan. This growth could have a significant impact on monetary policies in various nations. However, it seems that until the latter half of 2020, the public was largely unaware of the issue. In recent years, cryptocurrencies, particularly Bitcoin, have captured the headlines and public interest.

The BIS published a paper on central bank digital currencies in 2020 that included the findings of a survey they conducted regarding CBDC development. Table 3.1 indicates CBDCs launched or currently under development by central banks around the world. According to the poll, 86% of central banks are interested in the growth of CBDC.

Table 3.1: CBDCs under development (as of 2022).

No.	Country	CBDC
1	Bahamas	Sand Dollar
2	China	Digital yuan
3	Ecuador	Dinero electrónico
4	Eurozone	Digital euro
5	Japan	Digital yen
6	South Korea	Digital won
7	Russian Federation	Digital ruble
8	Singapore	Project Ubin
9	South Africa	Digital Rand
10	Sweden	e-krona
11	Thailand	Digital baht
12	Ukraine	e-hryvnia
13	United Kingdom	Digital pound
14	United States	Digital dollar
15	Uruguay	e-Peso

Source: Buchholz (July 21, 2022).

The following brief descriptions of the various stages of CBDC development have been provided by the Atlantic Council (2021) to help readers understand them better:
–   Research: Governments typically begin investigating CBDC developments in other countries during the research stage. Working groups are formed to carry out this kind of study, often researching project viability, CBDC implications, and use cases.
–   Pilot: A stage following the initial development phase, which could also be referred to as the preliminary testing phase. Pilot projects often involve evaluating CBDCs on a limited scale in a real-world setting, although the setting and participants are constrained.
–   Development: Following the completion of research and the recognition of the development's advantages, the development stage begins. It typically starts with the development of technologies on a small scale and continues with experiments in carefully monitored settings.
–   Inactive: Governments that are not currently developing CBDCs may have previously begun to investigate them but have left the initiative in place. They may wish to observe how development unfolds in other countries first.
–   Cancelled: Although research on CBDCs has been carried out, the government has rejected moving forward with the project and it has been abandoned.
–   Launched: CBDCs have entered the retail or wholesale market after completing their development and testing phases.

CBDCs can be released in two ways:
–   They can be created in retail form to be accessible to any user and functional for all transactions, or
–   they can be created in wholesale form, which is only accessible to financial institutions and interbank settlements. Therefore, the general public cannot access it.

Position of CBDCs in the Modern Payments System

It is important to note the primary attributes of the accepted forms of payment before discussing CBDCs' role in the contemporary payments system. Denmark's central bank created a chart in 2017 that outlines the key features of cash, bank deposits, CBDCs, and cryptocurrencies. According to Gürtler et al. (2017), only cash has a physical form (banknotes and coins), making it tangible. However, each payment method possesses both similar and unique characteristics. The most notable difference is that cryptocurrencies have no claims on anyone and are highly volatile.

According to the BIS (2020), central banks currently create two types of currency and support a third with infrastructure. They issue physical money, such as banknotes and coins, as well as digital deposits known as reserves or settlement balances.

Physical money is typically available to the general public, while electronic central bank reserves are typically only available to approved financial institutions.

Private money, such as commercial bank deposits, is the third type of currency, which is widely available through electronic means. Central banks assist commercial banks in various ways, including enabling interbank transactions with central bank money, allowing convertibility between commercial and central bank money through the issuance of banknotes, and providing supplementary liquidity through the role of lender of last resort. It is important to note that while cash and reserves are liabilities of the central bank, deposits in commercial banks are not. CBDCs would be a new form of currency issued by the government.

To better understand the contemporary payments system, the International Monetary Fund (IMF) has defined four key characteristics: (1) type, (2) value, (3) backstop and (4) technology.
1) Type refers to the actual medium of exchange, with cash being an example of an object-based payment settled immediately and claims-based payments requiring a more intricate infrastructure.
2) Value refers to the fixed or variable redemption of payment methods.
3) Backstop refers to whether the government guarantees redemption or if it is primarily based on commercial and legal norms.
4) Technology refers to the centralized or decentralized nature of transactions.

The Concept of Central Bank Digital Currencies

In order to understand the potential implications of CBDCs on the current payments system, it is important to examine the underlying concepts and proposed functions of these digital currencies. By delving deeper into the advantages and disadvantages of CBDCs compared to traditional fiat money, we can gain a better understanding of their potential role in the financial system.

Conceptual Framework

According to Mancini-Griffoli et al. (2018), there are two perspectives from which to view the benefits of CBDCs:
– The consumer or demand side considers how CBDCs may eliminate the need for physical money and improve the experience for users.
– The supply side looks at how CBDCs may enhance the effectiveness of central bank policies and respond to certain market failures.

However, it is important to also consider the potential trade-offs and expenses of implementing CBDCs. The primary objective of CBDCs is to enhance the current functions of money, which include:

- acting as a measuring tool for accounting purposes,
- facilitating transactions, and
- offering protection from different risks.

Features of CBDCs

The properties of CBDCs can be categorized into three primary groups: instrumental, system, and institutional.

Instrumental Attributes
- Digital form: Unlike physical cash, CBDCs are only available in digital form.
- Legal tender: The government has designated CBDCs as a type of money that can be used to settle obligations and taxes.
- Reserve support: CBDCs are supported by the reserves of the central bank, ensuring stability and credibility.
- Accessibility: Depending on how each CBDC is built, the public may have simple access to them.

System Attributes
- Interoperability: CBDCs may be made to work with current infrastructure and other digital payment systems.
- Scalability: CBDCs may be made to accommodate a high volume of transactions.
- Security: To combat fraud and hacking, CBDCs may be built with cutting-edge security features.
- Traceability: For anti-money laundering and counter-terrorist financing objectives, CBDCs can be built to enable transaction tracing.

Institutional Attributes
- Control by the central bank: The central bank issues and manages CBDCs, providing oversight and regulation.
- Tool for monetary policy: CBDCs can be a tool for monetary policy, enabling the central bank to modify the amount of money available to the economy.
- Financial inclusion: By granting underbanked communities access to digital currency, CBDCs can advance financial inclusion.
- Innovation: CBDCs can encourage innovation in the payments sector and create new openings for expansion and improvement.

Proposed Role in Terms of Consumers

According to Mancini-Griffoli et al. (2018), consumers aim to maximize their benefits while minimizing their expenses and risks. However, predicting the public's preferred global course for CBDCs is difficult as public interests can vary greatly between nations and even individuals. It is important to note that CBDCs may not always be superior to other forms of payment.

Adrian and Mancini-Griffoli (2019) at the IMF have proposed two possible designs for the conceptual framework of CBDCs. The first design, known as fixed design, would have no discretion by the reserve bank. CBDCs would be more beneficial for person-to-person, business-to-business, and consumer-to-consumer transactions due to minimal settlement risk and low transaction costs. Additionally, Adrian and Mancini-Griffoli predict that CBDCs would have lower default risk in various nations. However, this may not be accurate in all cases. Other payment methods may perform better in fixed designs where the cross-sell potential is limited and CBDCs lack additional features.

The second design, known as flexible design, would allow for CBDCs to provide superior interest yields. Additionally, CBDCs would be safer than conventional payment methods, particularly in terms of anonymity. However, anonymity may also increase the risk of loss and theft and may not be well received by central banks. Only under strict conditions and with minimal restrictions on CBDC holdings would they be able to provide complete transaction anonymity.

According to Adrian and Mancini-Griffoli the demand for CBDCs will be driven by their design. The demand and interest in CBDCs may vary depending on the design and location. While CBDCs may be superior in some areas of the financial system, there may still be better ways to make payments. Mancini-Griffoli et al. (2018) state that CBDCs could eventually replace paper bills but may be more appealing in nations with low banking adoption and inadequate resolution platforms, particularly in the absence of stored value capabilities. The success of CBDCs will ultimately be determined by the government, jurisdiction, and design.

Accounting Treatment for CBDCs

CBDCs would be treated in accounting terms in a manner akin to that of conventional fiat money. Since the CBDC represents a claim by the holder against the central bank, it would be recorded as a liability on the central bank's balance sheet. Any assets that are used to support the CBDC, such as foreign exchange reserves or government bonds, would also need to be recorded by the central bank. The accounting treatment of CBDC by various entities should follow the following principles:
- Commercial banks would record CBDCs as a liability if they held it as a deposit.
- Holding CBDCs would be reflected as an asset on the balance sheet of both individuals and companies.

- If a business uses a CBDC to purchase goods or services from another business, the transaction would be recorded in the same way as a traditional fiat currency transaction. The business would debit its cash or bank account and credit its accounts payable or expense account.

Journal Entry for Businesses

The journal entry for a business using CBDCs to purchase goods or services would typically involve a debit to the cash or bank account and a credit to the accounts payable or expense account. For example, if a business purchases $100 worth of goods from a supplier using a CBDC, the journal entry would be:

Debit: Cash (or CBDC account) $100
Credit: Accounts payable $100

This journal entry records the fact that the business has used $100 of its cash or CBDC to pay for goods it has received from the supplier, and the supplier now has a $100 claim (accounts payable) on the business.

Journal Entry for Central Bank

A central bank would include the transaction in its balance sheet when it issued a CBDC. The specifics of the CBDC issuance and the assets being used to back it would determine the journal entry, but an example of a general journal entry would be:

Debit: $1 billion from the CBDC liability account (for instance, if 1 billion units of CBDC with a $1 each are issued)
Credit: $1,000,000,000 in assets (such as foreign exchange reserves or government bonds)

For example, assume the central bank has issued 1 billion units of CBDC, each worth $1, and these units are backed by assets like foreign exchange reserves or government bonds, according to this journal entry. A digital representation of a nation's fiat currency that is issued and supported by the central bank is known as a CBDC. Businesses that accept CBDCs as payment must account for it similarly to how they currently account for other forms of currency in their financial statements.

A CBDC would be listed as a cash asset on the balance sheet alongside other forms of cash and cash equivalents like bank deposits. Any income or expenses related to CBDC transactions would also need to be included in the income statement.

Disclosure of CBDC-Based Transactions for Companies

In order to provide more information and transparency to investors, companies may also need to disclose their CBDC holdings and transactions in the notes to the financial statements.

- Balance sheet: CBDC would be listed as a cash asset alongside other types of cash and cash equivalents like bank deposits on the balance sheet. An organization might have $600,000 in cash and cash equivalents on its balance sheet if, for instance, it has $100,000 in CBDC and $500,000 in bank deposits.
- Income statement: Any revenue or costs associated with CBDC transactions would be recorded on the income statement. The sale of goods or services for $50,000 in CBDC, for instance, would be counted as revenue. Expenses would be recorded if the company paid fees for converting CBDC to other currencies or other costs associated with CBDC transactions.
- Notes to the financial statements: Companies may be required to provide additional information about their CBDC holdings and transactions in the notes to the financial statements. They might be required to provide information such as the total amount of CBDC held at the end of the reporting period as well as any changes to the holdings' value during that time. They might also be required to disclose any significant limitations on the use of CBDC as well as any material risks related to holding CBDC.

Disclosure of CBDC-Based Transactions for Central Banks

A central bank is required to disclose its financial statements to the general public and interested parties, just like any other financial institution. A central bank's financial position, performance, and cash flows are displayed in the financial statements.

A central bank would list the value of the CBDC it has issued as a liability alongside other types of liabilities like banknotes and coins in circulation on the balance sheet. Any income or expenses related to CBDC transactions would also need to be included in the income statement.

To give investors and other stakeholders more information and transparency, a central bank may also be required to disclose its CBDC holdings and transactions in the notes to the financial statements. Depending on the specific rules and recommendations issued by the central bank and accounting standards boards, the precise accounting treatment of CBDC may change.

A central bank may list any interest paid on CBDC held by commercial banks as an expense on the income statement and the issuance of CBDC as an increase in liabilities on the balance sheet. Since the central bank serves as a lender of last resort and has different obligations, its balance sheet differs from that of a commercial bank. In order to meet the demand for money, the central bank must hold assets that can be quickly converted into cash, such as government bonds.

CBDCs' Role in the Banking System

Central banks, being on the supply side of CBDCs, control the functions of money and distribute it to customers. According to Mancini-Griffoli et al. (2018), central banks have two main roles:
- to take care of their customers by designing the currency, and
- to ensure that the currency complies with established societal standards.

The majority of currencies issued by central banks serve three main purposes, as stated by Adrian and Mancini-Griffoli (2019):
- units of account,
- means of payment, and
- store of value.

It is important for central banks to ensure that the deployment of CBDCs does not result in an unsustainable monetary policy that undermines other monetary public policies, such as monetary policy effectiveness, financial stability, and financial integrity. CBDCs may assist in resolving challenges with financial intermediation, particularly in emerging countires, as per Adrian and Mancini-Griffoli. However, it is important to note that CBDCs may not be able to resolve the conflict between encouraging financial intermediation and providing a safe place to deposit value, which generally refers to the expansion of specific financial solutions that charge for intermediation and provide a safe place to deposit value, as per Adrian and Mancini-Griffoli.

Combining liquidity reserves that businesses and families keep on hand to handle payment disruptions is a way to deal with potential payment disruptions. Additionally, since most shocks do not occur in one go, they can borrow some of the money while holding only a small share in highly liquid and secure assets. According to Mancini-Griffoli, central banks should strive to buck this trend, but CBDCs may not be useful in this regard. CBDCs must also be fully prefunded, similar to narrow financing solutions. CBDCs' fast payment system can only assist fractional reserve banks by providing a competitive service compared to alternative value storage options.

According to Bech et al. (2018), the decline in the use of cash is already apparent and will only continue on this trajectory. Sweden is one of the most prominent examples, where the use of cash has significantly decreased, and people are increasingly using digital payment methods. However, according to Bech, the use of cash appears to be increasing in several countries, such as Hong Kong and Japan, though this may not be entirely accurate as growth is measured as a percentage of GDP. It is clear that some businesses have changed and are no longer accepting cash payments; instead, most of them now offer credit card payment options.

Scenarios of CBDCs' Adoption

According to Adrian and Mancini-Griffoli (2019) in their paper *The Rise of Digital Money*, there are three potential scenarios for central banks to implement when using CBDCs. These scenarios are similar to those previously outlined by the BIS, but Adrian and Mancini-Griffoli provide a more detailed discussion of each possibility. These scenarios primarily focus on the integration of fiat and digital currencies. However, this is one of the main challenges that central banks must overcome as they must decide whether to preserve the fiat currency, completely replace it, or maintain both currencies in parallel with the implementation of CBDCs.

Coexistence

According to Bech et al. (2018), the most likely scenario for the incorporation of CBDCs into the financial system is coexistence. They believe that it is the most likely outcome. Additionally, e-money suppliers recycle a lot of customer funds back to banks in the form of certificates of deposit or other types of short-term financing. According to Adrian and Mancini-Griffoli, the optimal solution for CBDC incorporation into the financial system would not be through financial institutions.

Banks would face negative impacts, such as switching from profitable retail funding to riskier and more expensive wholesale funding, losing transaction records, and a lack of customer interaction. Smaller banks would be particularly vulnerable to potential significant funding fluctuations. Adrian and Mancini-Griffoli predict that banks may respond by offering higher interest rates, improving their current services, or seeking alternative funding sources, with the first two options primarily focused on retaining customers and deposits.

Complementarity

Adrian and Mancini-Griffoli argue that this concept would work particularly well in developing markets. E-money, in particular, could facilitate the migration of less affluent individuals and small enterprises from cash payments to more complex financial services, such as credit, savings tools, accounting services, and assistance from commercial banks. Additionally, it could introduce these populations to new technology.

However, Adrian and Mancini-Griffoli also note that a complementary situation may also be beneficial in advanced economies. Banks in developed nations may benefit from the adoption of digital currencies, as they would be able to access information that would enable them to assess the creditworthiness of their clients.

Takeover

Adrian and Mancini-Griffoli identify takeover as a final potential scenario for CBDCs. This would be the most drastic course of action and would require a significant overhaul of the entire banking sector. Given that credit is increasingly being mediated by markets in the current banking model – which relies heavily on wholesale funding – this scenario is unlikely, but Adrian and Mancini-Griffoli argue that economies should be prepared for it in case it materializes in the future.

Adrian and Mancini-Griffoli propose that consumer deposits could be converted to digital currencies or held in foreign Central Bank currency or government bonds in a takeover scenario. This strategy would limit the potential of fractional banking, which enables banks to accept deposits and retain only a small portion of them as liquid assets, such as government bonds and central bank reserves, while lending the remainder to individuals and businesses to promote economic growth.

However, it is important to consider that this approach would leave several areas unaddressed and conventional banks may resist this change. A major concern is the potential impact on liquidity and the availability of funds for lending to the private sector, particularly in regard to uninsured deposits. Additionally, there are unexplored areas such as mortgages, loan extensions, and funding that need to be integrated into CBDCs, raising questions about the security of these banking services.

Given the complexity and potential challenges of implementing a takeover scenario, Adrian and Mancini-Griffoli stress the importance of thoroughly examining the possible implications and addressing these issues. This is necessary to create a better financial product, and ultimately develop an effective policy that can be integrated into the existing financial system.

Synthetic Central Bank Digital Currencies

A synthetic CBDC is a public-private partnership that promotes competition and preserves the competitive advantages of e-money providers. In this model, the private sector focuses on providing excellent customer service, designing user-friendly interfaces, and fostering innovation, while the public sector remains responsible for ensuring trust.

By incorporating the advantages of both CBDCs and public-private partnerships, a synthetic CBDC would offer the best of both worlds and potentially facilitate a smoother integration of CBDCs into the international financial system. However, it should be noted that as synthetic CBDCs are a distinct topic, they will not be further discussed in this study.

Challenges

The integration of CBDCs into the financial system may offer numerous advantages and potential benefits. However, before a complete integration of the future financial system can be achieved, a number of obstacles must be overcome. These include regulatory, legal, cybersecurity, privacy, stability, financial inclusion, and currency resilience challenges, which are considered the most critical.

Legal and Regulatory Approaches

Regulatory reactions to cryptocurrencies have been observed to vary widely between countries, with the United States serving as an example of how they can differ even within the same country." The regulatory approval of CBDCs may encounter a similar fate. While most financial institutions are unlikely to offer CBDCs in the near future, some are conducting further research and evaluating their options. It is expected that as more central banks adopt CBDCs after the demonstration of their efficacy, more will follow suit. Boar and Wehrli (2021) also mention that the COVID-19 pandemic of 2020 has generated new incentives for CBDC development, which will likely lead to quicker legal and regulatory clearance in the future.

   The current focus is on a more in-depth examination of the potential legal and regulatory environment for CBDCs. According to Boar and Wehrli, the law related to CBDC is often based on an existing legal framework, which includes the Consumer Protection Act, the Budget Act, the Financial Integrity Act, and the central bank's governing legislation. Each central bank has its own organizational structure; thus, it is the responsibility of each national central bank to determine whether the regulatory environment allows for the issuance of CBDCs.

   Additionally, indirect factors must also be considered, such as the government's ability to enforce requirements, the need for monitoring, and the security of sensitive data and information technology. As previously mentioned by Mancini-Griffoli et al. (2018), a change in the law may be required to permit the issue of CBDCs. It is important to note that certain terms may have different meanings in different countries. Typically, the term "legal tender" refers to government-issued money. However, it should be noted that a creditor is not necessarily required to accept legal tender as payment, and thus, the precise meaning of legal tender may vary by country. Ultimately, the ability of a sovereign state to create a legislative framework for the central issuance of coins and banknotes is essential to the legal concept of money.

   Mancini-Griffoli note that as the concept of legal tender evolves, central banks must address two key concerns. One concern is to include CBDCs sold at retail within the definition of legal tender. There is a high probability that retail CBDCs denominated in the local currency will be considered legal tender in a particular country. However, if retail CBDCs are denominated in a currency other than the domestic currency, the relevant government or jurisdiction must recognize them as legal tender in order for them to be used for debt settlement.

Another concern is to enhance the understanding of the concept of legal tender. Several central banks have chosen to conduct further research on how retail CBDCs differ from current systems and whether new central bank legislation is required to create digital central bank money.

Issue of Privacy

The primary issue is that compliance with the law would make it unlawful to provide the same level of anonymity for virtual currency as for real cash. If total anonymity is provided, banking institutions cannot combat organized crime and money laundering since they cannot identify consumers. Kaminska (2020) contends that central banks that issue CBDCs will not act as impartial infrastructure providers. Instead, they would compete under their separate legal frameworks and administrative systems to become the leading issuers. The mistrust of the central bank by consumers would impede CBDC development and monetary system unification.

CBDCs' Currency Stability Compared to Fiat Currency

The stability of CBDCs and fiat currencies is a topic of ongoing debate. The stability of currency is a key function of cash, and verifying the dependability of CBDCs as a digital technology is crucial. According to Mancini-Griffoli, maintaining price stability for CBDCs in the near future will be challenging. The global financial crisis and COVID-19 pandemic have highlighted how a central bank's ability to determine interest rates may be impacted by the availability of cash. However, Mancini-Griffoli argue that cash will continue to be used for the foreseeable future and that CBDCs will not replace cash instantly. Only if CBDCs are widely adopted will currency be phased out.

Adrian and Mancini-Griffoli (2019) have also examined alternative payment channels for CBDCs. They argue that CBDCs are functionally similar to cash or central bank money, making them an excellent store of value under normal conditions. However, concerns regarding operations and cybersecurity pose a risk to digital currency. These hazards are inherent to all alternative transaction methods. In addition to these two major risks, Adrian and Mancini-Griffoli identify four additional issues for CBDCs: liquidity risk, market risk, foreign currency risk, and default risk. They provide four solutions to these issues, which include investing in short-term government bonds, controlling the issuance of electronic money, reinvesting in firm assets, and increasing the capital of CBDC issuers.
- Liquidity risk: The risk of liquidity refers to the potential delay between the moment an issuer of digital currency receives a redemption request and the time the

agreed-upon amount is paid out. This risk is dependent on various factors, with market liquidity and the issuer's ability to repay being the most critical.

–   Market risk: On the other hand, market risk pertains to the potential for fluctuations in the market value of the digital currency service's holdings. Redemptions may be at risk if the issuer of the digital currency incurs significant financial losses.

–   Foreign currency risk: This arises when claims made with digital currency are denominated in a currency other than the country's unit of account. In such a scenario, the value of such claims may fluctuate based on fluctuations in the value of the foreign currency. Digital currency issuers who manage a basket of currencies may be able to mitigate this risk.

–   Default risk: This occurs when an issuer of digital currency is unable to meet its debt commitments or incurs losses during regular business operations. As a result, debt collectors may attempt to recover funds directly from clients.

To address these issues, Adrian and Mancini-Griffoli provided four solutions. These strategies may reduce hazards and increase CBDC stability, stabilizing cryptocurrencies in the same way as traditional cash.

–   The first strategy emphasizes financial investments, where central banks could acquire more short-term government bonds.

–   The second recommendation is to create CBDCs, or digital currencies, where central banks should control the formation of electronic money so that it never exceeds the total amount of client payments received.

–   The third strategy is reinvesting in firm assets.

–   The fourth strategy is to increase the capital of CBDCs and their issuers to compensate for market losses and unexpected movements that may otherwise undermine stability.

CBDCs and Financial Inclusion

According to Boar et al. (2020), the expansion of CBDCs represents the realization of several objectives for central banks, and the incentives for doing so vary considerably. They argue that the most apparent contrasts exist between developing and established economies, and central banks themselves may demonstrate significant diversity. The fundamental motivation for the creation of CBDCs is their potential utility as a medium of exchange. However, it is essential to keep in mind that the proliferation of CBDCs will have both benefits and drawbacks.

However, concerns about data protection, digital literacy, IT access, and trust may jeopardize the advancement of digitalization for certain users. The authors warn that if the growth of CBDCs is not addressed thoroughly, further financial exclusion may develop, particularly in less developed regions where digital services, such as internet access, data privacy, hardware, and support, are difficult to obtain. Boar argue that emerging markets represent a potential opportunity for the expansion of access to financial services afforded by CBDCs.

Risks to Financial Intermediation

It is widely acknowledged that CBDCs pose a potential threat to the stability of the financial system and may decrease the availability of credit to the economy if they are utilized as a replacement for bank deposits and payment activities. However, recent studies suggest that this perspective is inadequate and that the implications for the financial services industry could be manageable.

Firstly, the actions of central banks may play a significant role in determining the risks associated with CBDCs. To preserve the benefits of their status as primary providers of financial services, central banks may opt to delegate the distribution of CBDCs to other types of financial intermediaries. Central banks must also consider the potential demand for CBDCs and may adjust key aspects of the CBDC design to mitigate risks. For example, the implementation of tiered compensation systems and holding restrictions may effectively reduce risks. Additionally, central banks may provide significant amounts of liquidity to alleviate constraints caused by expected changes in the composition of bank financing. Research suggests that these changes would have a minimal impact on the allocation of capital.

In addition to these considerations, the issuance of CBDCs may also have positive impacts on the overall economy. As the demand for cash decreases, CBDCs may be created to ensure that the sovereign nation's currency remains the standard against which all other forms of private currency are measured. Furthermore, capital allocation may benefit from the use of CBDCs due to lower transaction fees and improved payment simplicity (Assenmacher et al., 2021; Keister and Sanches, 2019). The dominance of traditional banks in the financial market may also be eroded, leading to increased competition (Andolfatto, 2020). Additionally, CBDCs may provide advanced payment solutions, allowing traditional financial institutions to compete with newer players in the industry, such as large technology companies.

CBDCs has the potential to encourage bank intermediation. In an effort to compensate for lost revenue, banks may have to increase the amount of money paid to depositors. This would increase both the use of CBDCs and deposit balances, and result in an increase in lending activities. CBDCs may fill the gap created by the decline in cash usage by providing an alternative to rate floors and deposits, thereby reducing the monopolistic profits of banks and encouraging them to lend more (Chiu and Rivadeneyra, 2021).

CBDCs Supporting Technology Overview

The fundamental functionality of CBDCs necessitates the implementation of corresponding backend technologies. In order to fully utilize their essential capabilities, CBDCs require a robust technological foundation. According to the BIS (2020), the development of CBDC technology must be fully functional across a range of use cases before it can be considered complete. To enhance understanding of CBDC technologies, the BIS (2020) has compiled a description of their most crucial characteristics and technical challenges. The technological aspects of CBDCs include:

– Secure and efficient digital storage: CBDCs require a secure and efficient way to store digital currencies, such as using blockchain technology or other distributed ledger systems.
– Scalability: The CBDC system must be able to handle large volumes of transactions, especially during peak usage times.
– Interoperability: The CBDC system should be able to interact with other systems, such as existing payment infrastructure, to ensure seamless integration.
– Privacy and security: CBDCs must provide strong privacy and security features to protect users' financial data and prevent fraud.
– Accessibility: The system must be accessible to all users, regardless of their location or device, and must be usable by people with different levels of digital literacy.
– Anonymity: The system should provide anonymity when it is necessary.
– Auditability: The system should be auditable, in order to detect and prevent fraud.
– Governance: The system should have a governance structure that provides oversight and ensures the system's integrity.
– Resilience: The system should be able to withstand and recover from technical failures, cyberattacks, and other disruptions.
– Compliance: The system should comply with regulatory requirements and standards.

Advantages of CBDCs

The expansion of CBDCs presents several advantages for central banks, with varying incentives for implementation. These include:

– Reduced transaction costs: CBDCs may facilitate faster institutional and retail payments and reduce transaction fees.
– Enhanced economic growth: Supporting economic growth and digital innovation is a primary objective of CBDCs. They have the potential to establish a trustworthy digital currency jurisdiction and an attractive crypto environment, thereby promoting economic activity and technological development.

- Cost-effectiveness: CBDCs offer a lower cost factor as there are no manufacturing, storage, shipping, or disposal expenses. Additionally, they provide secure distribution channels and alleviate concerns about fraud in the financial system.
- Liquidity: CBDCs have the ability to provide temporary liquidity assistance, which can be useful in times of bank holidays. This can assist in reducing the risk of systemic processes caused by different institutions.
- Financial inclusion: CBDCs have the potential to provide access to digital payment systems for the majority of unbanked clients, enabling them to access low-cost or free contemporary digital payment alternatives.
- Competition of payment systems: CBDCs may promote competition in the financial sector and incentivize private players to innovate.
- Payment tracking: The absence of intermediaries in CBDC transactions allows for more precise tracking of payments and can reduce settlement periods.

Disadvantages of CBDCs

- As CBDCs offer an alternate means of keeping and transmitting money, they may cause disruption in the established banking system.
- A CBDC would require users to give their name and transaction history to the central bank, which might raise concerns about privacy and monitoring.
- As digital currencies are frequently held in online wallets and are susceptible to hacking efforts, their use may raise the danger of cyberattacks.
- Those without access to digital technology or those who lack computer literacy may not be able to use CBDCs, resulting in a gap in the availability of CBDCs.

Cybersecurity Risks affecting CBDCs

Cybersecurity problems, data breaches account, theft, counterfeiting, and even further-reaching difficulties linked with quantum computing are all real threats to CBDCs, as they are to any digital payment system. Before CBDCs become widely accepted, individuals must feel secure using them. A failure to examine and engage in a robust cybersecurity strategy will render them ineffective. How can we ensure that CBDCs will be there for the long haul? There are four crucial cybersecurity areas to consider.

CBDC Credential Loss and Theft

The loss or theft of CBDC credentials can impede access to funds and their transfer. For example, a passphrase that may be conveyed through paper or a hardware token containing private keys might be used as credentials. The danger of theft and credential loss is widespread and severe, placing account funds and data at risk.

Passwords are particularly susceptible to both online and offline attack vectors. Today, hackers may utilize social engineering, side-channel attacks, and malware to gain access to the credentials of a CBDC user. Furthermore, if their hardware tokens or passcodes are lost or destroyed due to fire or water, CBDC customers should not lose all of their assets and data. Lost credentials must be recoverable within the system.

A CBDC built on blockchain technology might utilize a multi-signature (multi-sig) wallet, where at least one of the following replications (the central bank and/or the end user's family) has credentials to the same wallet. With a multi-sig wallet, multiple users must coordinate on every transaction. Even in online banking, where two-factor authentication (2FA) is prevalent, such security-usability compromises are widespread. If the infrastructure supporting CBDCs is obsolete, a trusted insider might simply update a database record holding sensitive information by substituting the corresponding credentials.

Privileged Role of Users

Depending on the consensus protocol employed, non-central bank nodes with privileged authority could declare transactions invalid, preventing them from being accepted by the network, resulting in a denial-of-service attack and censorship of CBDC customers.

A pertinent concern is the potential for privileged actions by central bank or government insiders, law enforcement, and other agents in relation to CBDC accounts, such as the ability to freeze or withdraw funds without user consent. While such capabilities may align with current compliance procedures in regulated payment systems, they also raise the possibility of abuse by malicious insiders. As with any form of information security, it is imperative for the central bank and any intermediaries involved to have a robust cybersecurity risk-management plan in place to address these privileges. Employing multi-party mechanisms, akin to those utilized by multi-signature wallets or other protective measures, may heighten the difficulty of such attacks.

Furthermore, if the CBDC operates on blockchain technology and involves nodes from non-central bank entities with validation or invalidation powers for transactions, there is a potential security risk from malicious validator nodes. These nodes could pose threats to the system's security and undermine the central bank's monetary authority and independence by accepting or rejecting transactions contrary to the central bank's intention. Therefore, it is generally advised against granting transaction validation powers to non-central bank nodes unless deemed absolutely necessary.

Quantum Computing

The impact of quantum computing on the encryption algorithms and cryptographic data structures used to protect data access, confidentiality, and integrity will eventually affect all financial services, including CBDCs. Therefore, in order to maintain the security of CBDC accounts, the potential threat posed by future quantum computers must be considered throughout the technical development process. Financial institutions, such as central banks, must evaluate the vulnerability of their current systems in light of the impending age of quantum computing and plan accordingly. Additionally, future quantum computers may have the ability to bypass the CBDC system's encryption undetected.

In the context of CBDCs, it is crucial that cybersecurity, technical resilience, and effective technical governance are given the utmost importance. The security and integrity of citizen data and finances, the efficacy of the CBDC program, the reputational risk of the central bank, and the public perception of the new currency may be compromised without a well-executed cybersecurity policy that addresses the aforementioned threats. Thus, to ensure the system's continuous functioning and integrity, a comprehensive approach that addresses a broad range of possible threats must be implemented. This is a fundamental requirement for the success of CBDCs.

Privacy

Privacy is a significant concern with regard to federal CBDC accounts, as they may provide the government with unprecedented access to personal bank transaction data, which has been a major source of disagreement throughout the development process. A government's decision to create a CBDC must strike a balance between the right of individuals to privacy and the need to curb illegal financial activities. The US Privacy Act of 1974 currently governs the government's access to personal data; however, this law was created in a different era of payment processing and, therefore, may need to be revised.

Perhaps technological advancements can assist in finding a compromise between these conflicting aims. However, if the government insists on its "need to know," technical measures alone may not be sufficient to prevent the abuse of information. The public has yet to be convinced that the correct balance has been struck between the amount of information the public needs and the amount of information that should be kept private. The advent of CBDCs and digital currencies in general may be one solution.

Even if privacy-enhancing technologies are implemented, the political challenge of determining the rules under which a CBDC would operate remains. The Fed believes that all CBDCs should comply with the most recent anti-money laundering and counter-terrorist financing regulations. However, the US Congress has the authority to modify or remove these limitations, as it has the final say on whether or not the Fed may issue CBDCs. Before the Fed issues a CBDC, which raises serious privacy concerns, a more in-depth debate on how privacy in financial services can and should be protected legally, rather than solely through technical means, must take place.

CBDCs as a Potential Replacement of Cash

As the adoption of modern technologies increases, so too does the evolution of monetary systems and the institutions that support them. In recent years, the proliferation of online payment systems has been facilitated by long-awaited infrastructural advancements. Over the past few decades, central banks around the globe have adopted real-time gross settlement (RTGS) systems. At present, more than 55 nations have implemented retail fast payment systems (FPSs), which enable instantaneous money transfers between customers and businesses 24/7. These FPSs also contribute to the maintenance of a thriving ecosystem of private and alternative payment service providers (PSPs). Examples include the TARGET2, the Eurozone's RTGS system, the Unified Payments Interface in India, CoDi in Mexico, Pix in Brazil, and FedNow in the United States. These developments suggest that access to reliable government-issued money may foster creativity and innovation.

However, there are proposals for fundamental changes to the current monetary system. An ongoing COVID-19 pandemic could necessitate cashless transactions and a surge in digital payments in the retail industry. Central banks are developing CBDCs to more accurately reflect central bank money in the digital economy, in addition to incremental but steady progress. CBDCs have the potential to foster future innovations that accelerate, simplify, and secure the financial system. Research into CBDCs allows for the examination and improvement of the public interest argument for digital currencies. The monetary system plays a crucial role in facilitating commerce and is deeply ingrained in people's daily lives; it serves a vital societal function. The market structure and governance arrangements that facilitate technological advances in money and payments will determine the ultimate impact on the well-being of a society's citizens. The same technology that increases access, competition, and fresh ideas may also foster market dominance and the hoarding of sensitive information. Ultimately, the outcome will depend on whether the regulations governing the payment system provide competitors with open payment platforms and a level playing field.

As the world becomes increasingly digitized, it is becoming increasingly imperative for central banks to engage in the development of CBDCs. In recent years, a number of fascinating new opportunities for the growth of digital currencies have emerged. One such opportunity is the rising popularity of Bitcoin and other cryptocurrencies, which, despite being speculative assets rather than currency, are increasingly being used to facilitate money laundering, ransomware attacks, and other forms of financial crime. Another opportunity is the controversy surrounding stablecoins, which are digital assets that are pegged to the value of a stable fiat currency. Stablecoins have the potential to damage the cohesiveness and liquidity of the monetary system and are seen as merely a complement to the present monetary system rather than a game changer.

A third opportunity is the entrance of major technology companies into the financial services and payment services industries. These companies have a significant competitive advantage due to the intensity of network effects, which are created by the large number of existing users on a platform and the greater likelihood that a potential new user will choose to join that platform. However, there is a possibility that network effects may not always benefit customers and may result in increased market dominance and the hoarding of sensitive information.

The high cost of linked services is one of the most important difficulties with the existing payment system, which may be exacerbated by market dominance and consolidation. Traditional digital payment methods, such as credit and debit cards, remain more expensive than cash, despite decades of technological breakthroughs that have significantly reduced the cost of transmission equipment and bandwidth. The high transaction fees associated with digital payment options may be attributed to their limited availability.

Inclusion of Commercial Banks into the CBDC Scheme

For an effective rollout of CBDCs, it is essential to establish public-private partnerships. Such alliances will enable central banks to leverage existing infrastructure and consumer connections, thereby facilitating the implementation of use cases that meet the needs of end users. To increase the likelihood of widespread adoption by commercial banks and other private stakeholders, such as technology enablers, retailers, and buyers, central banks should involve them in the launch process.

It is likely that other nations will seek CBDC models that are tailored to their own specific needs, resources, and constituencies. Therefore, foreign and local financial institutions must disclose their CBDC policies and exchange information with other national central banks in a multi-model environment.

CBDCs offer significant potential and an increasing number of central banks are exploring their adoption options. However, there are several challenges that must be overcome, including the impact on financial markets, regulation, and the actions of commercial banks, as well as data security and privacy. In many of the world's leading nations, the real economy has traditionally been supported by the conventional two-tier banking system.

To maintain confidence between state-owned central banks and private commercial banks, the banking system and the design of CBDCs must be taken into consideration. Notably, commercial banks and financial services providers should issue wallets that manage CBDCs, while central banks should issue the value and guarantee its legitimacy.

Maintaining the Two-Tier System

Central banks and commercial banks have a long-standing history of cooperation, with central banks responsible for macroeconomic issues, such as monetary policy and currency stability, while commercial banks provide services, such as customer counseling, lending, and corporate finance.

In the context of CBDCs, this balance between the two is both viable and desirable. Central banks will be responsible for the issuance and distribution of digital money, while private banks will play a crucial role in its circulation. Similar to the fiat currency currently in use, commercial institutions will be responsible for distribution and customer engagement. Additionally, CBDCs can offer financial services and solutions that are at the forefront of innovation.

In the future, these traditional roles will remain unchanged, but commercial banks will also have the opportunity to advance in their roles as service providers. With the implementation of a generic CBDC, new digital business models, as well as income and growth potential, may become accessible. For example, the integration and utilization of advanced automation in online shopping, through the use of value chains and smart contracts, can ensure that pre-agreed actions are carried out in response to predefined events.

There is no cause for concern regarding competition from central banks, as the existing division of responsibilities and duties among central banks, client banks, and financial services providers remains intact. By providing specialized applications for the use and safekeeping of CBDCs and building linkages to new CBDC-based customer services, commercial banks may potentially take advantage of the emergence of a digital central bank currency to further strengthen their relationships with clients.

Programming CBDCs to Support Commercial Banks

Commercial banks have the potential to create innovative new services and maintain their relevance in the digital era through the proper implementation of CBDCs. As the custodians of the majority of the world's currency supply, commercial banks have already begun to digitalize money.

For instance, CBDCs can leverage programmable features that are available at the level of commercial banks, allowing these institutions greater control over the CBDC environment and improving its performance while making it simpler for them to use. The provision of essential financial infrastructure by central banks acts as a driving force in the development of digital technologies. Business organizations may set additional requirements to protect the security of intelligent digital wallets.

Users of smart digital wallets can enforce regional laws by setting spending limits for children or setting up family-specific wallets. The advantages of a token-based

CBDC can be combined with the convenience of a traditional wallet. This design is appropriate for the current digital era and may promote financial inclusion.

CBDCs' Impact on the Global Financial System

The success of a CBDC in the retail market is dependent on the effective division of responsibilities between the private sector and the central bank. Through the formation of public-private partnerships, CBDCs can facilitate a new era of equal distribution of public and private monies, while also boosting productivity and maintaining the ability of central banks to conduct monetary policy and maintain financial stability.

However, there are arguments against single-layer, centrally controlled systems, such as direct CBDCs, as they would entail a significant transfer of operational responsibilities and costs from the private sector to the public sector, potentially weakening the central bank's role in formulating monetary policy. Innovation in the financial industry is constantly evolving, with banks, FinTechs, and big tech firms being well suited to spearhead cutting-edge developments. Central banks should actively assist these advancements rather than seeking to suppress them.

A two-tiered structure that separates the responsibilities of the public and private sectors is the most effective approach for CBDCs. Non-bank payment service providers (PSPs) and commercial banks that provide retail services should be given the bulk of operational labor and customer-facing responsibilities, while the central bank focuses on the system's core functions. This approach ensures that the system as a whole is secure, the money supply is flexible, and principles are upheld.

However, as residents and companies in a CBDC with a retail component have claims on the central bank, the central bank may have to become involved in commercial matters. It is essential to determine where the responsibility of the central bank ends and that of PSPs begins in terms of governance and control over data.

According to one proposed model for structuring CBDCs, the private sector would be responsible for managing retail payments in real time, as well as onboarding new customers and ensuring compliance with anti-money laundering and counter-terrorist financing requirements. Meanwhile, the central bank would maintain records on individual bank accounts. This "hybrid" organizational structure could facilitate CBDCs' ability to prop up the financial system, as the central bank would be able to obtain all necessary data to keep the payment system running, including customer balances, in the event of a payment service provider (PSP) failure. One example of this is the e-CNY, a hybrid currency that has been issued and is currently undergoing testing by the People's Bank of China.

Each CBDC technology solution must include a centralized digital ledger for tracking payment amounts and dates, as the ledger serves as the permanent record of all economic transactions. The question of whether a CBDC requires a trustworthy central authority to record the transactions ledger or a decentralized governance structure is crucial as money is considered the economy's memory. Under a hybrid or intermediated architecture, the central bank has the option of maintaining its own communications, record-keeping, and other tasks infrastructure or outsourcing these to a private sector source.

The Ideal Form of CBDC for Future Use

Due to digitization and decentralization, the financial sector is changing quickly. Both optimism and fear are generated by the thought that these innovations may decrease transaction costs and frictions, increase competition, and broaden consumers' access to financial services. We cannot afford to conceive just in terms of the present financial system, given that technological progress is the key engine of fundamental change.

The Development of Finance Decentralization and Digitalization's Beneficial Effects

The utilization of new cryptographic assets based on blockchain and other distributed ledger technologies, as well as encryption, has seen a significant increase in recent years. In 2018, the market value of cryptocurrencies was around $100 billion, but by November 2021, it was projected to surpass $3 trillion.

Progress has also been made in the area of decentralized finance (DeFi) systems and associated Bitcoin finance infrastructure. However, traditional legal protections for investor and consumer protection, market integrity, and transparency may not apply to cryptocurrency platforms, which could allow for various activities such as lending, trading, and holding crypto-assets.

As the cryptocurrency market matures, stablecoins are becoming increasingly popular. From a low of $29 billion in January 2021, the supply of stablecoins has risen by a factor of six and continued to increase through January 2022. There is a particular focus on a small number of dollar-pegged stablecoins: The most valued stablecoin accounted for around half of the market in January 2022, while the top four currencies held nearly 90% of the market share. In addition to being used as collateral on DeFi and other crypto platforms, stablecoins also facilitate trading and monetization of Bitcoin holdings.

A number of issuers are hopeful that stablecoins will be integrated into mainstream financial infrastructure and used for everyday transactions on a global scale. As such, it is crucial to have effective risk management and governance systems in place and to ensure that reserve assets are of sufficient quality to avoid "run risk." When a sudden surge in demand to redeem the stable currency at par with the dollar, the issuer faces run risk if it is unable to do so in a timely and acceptable manner. When monetary settlement is unclear or delayed, settlement risk arises and must be managed. There is also risk to the entire financial system due to the potential failure or difficulties of a major currency exchange.

The growth of the crypto financial system over the years suggests it will continue to develop in ways that further its integration with the traditional financial system. Policymakers in numerous countries are struggling to understand and respond to shifts in the international financial system. Different legal and regulatory regimes across the world aim to address similar threats.

Preparing for the Payment System of the Future

In the United States, international wire transfers are often costly and time-consuming for many individuals due to a lack of access to electronic banking and payment systems. The rapid growth of the digital financial ecosystem is indicative of the fact that recent technical advancements have enabled the emergence of new and exciting opportunities. The potential impact of new forms of digital currency and crypto-assets, among others, on the Federal Reserve's goals of price stability, full employment, low inflation, and reliable payments, must be evaluated. A viable approach would be to investigate whether a CBDC can preserve some of the secure and effective elements of the current financial system while also fostering private sector innovations that are shaping the future landscape.

The public and private sectors of the American monetary system are mutually supportive in many ways. For over a century, the Federal Reserve has been working on initiatives such as Fedwire and FedNow to modernize and improve the architecture of the American payment system, thus providing a solid foundation for the dynamism of the private sector. By providing high-quality goods and services, private sector financial organizations, including banks and non-banks, have been able to meet the needs of customers and investors dealing in dollars. As a result, a flexible payment system that can cater to the needs of businesses, clients, and investors has been developed.

The private sector adds additional competitive pressures that drive efficiency, the creation of new products, and innovation, while the public sector oversees and regulates financial intermediaries, maintains key payment rails, and manages crucial financial market infrastructures. Responsible innovation can increase productivity, improve access to the financial system, reduce costs, protect consumers and investors, and preserve financial stability.

As we contemplate the various future phases of the financial system, it is essential to maintain public access to government-issued, risk-free money in the digital financial system, similar to the Federal Reserve's issuance of physical currency. The Federal Reserve Board evaluates the potential benefits, risks, and policy issues associated with the implementation of a CBDC in the United States. The report makes no specific legislative recommendations and does not specify when the Board will decide whether or not to launch a CBDC for the United States. The report presents four CBDC design options that would be most beneficial for the United States, based on the analysis of data. According to the guidelines, a CBDC must be secure to protect users' personal information, intermediary so that users can interact with financial institutions rather than the Federal Reserve, widely transferable to avoid payment system disruptions, and identity-verified to assist law enforcement in their efforts against money laundering and terrorism.

Stability of Finance

A thorough analysis of the impact on the stability of the financial system must be conducted in any review of a CBDC. This analysis should consider both the current state of the financial system and any potential future developments. Given the US Federal Reserve's mandate to promote financial stability, it is imperative to examine the design elements that ensure compatibility with existing systems of financial intermediation. Depending on the context, a CBDC may be as appealing as a medium of exchange and investment that it is considered legal tender in its own right. The risk-averse nature of CBDCs may also make them a more popular choice in times of crisis. Therefore, it is crucial to consider design elements and tools, such as making CBDCs interest-free and limiting the amount that can be held or transferred by an individual user, to mitigate potential risks.

International Considerations

The domestic economy is one aspect of the financial system's future that can be predicted with a high degree of accuracy. The US dollar is the most commonly used currency for international commerce, and its prominence in global currency exchanges is influenced by several factors. It is important to consider the potential impact on global financial markets if the United States issues a CBDC without first assessing how other major countries might choose to issue CBDCs. Analyzing the potential effects on international financial markets and transactions, both with and without the US Federal Reserve's CBDC, is crucial. For example, the People's Bank of China has been testing the electronic Chinese yuan (e-CNY) in various Chinese regions over the past two years. The rapid early growth of the digital yuan may have long-term implications for monetary and commercial systems around the world, and the development of laws governing global electronic financial transactions may also be affected.

Technical Experimentation and Research

The Federal Reserve, in order to fulfill its mandate of promoting a secure, efficient, and inclusive system for US dollar transactions, must actively engage with the underlying technology of the digital financial system. This is due to the vast array of potential future outcomes, which may include a significant digitalization of the financial system

As the traditional financial system and the rapidly evolving digital financial system become increasingly integrated, it is crucial that the Federal Reserve Board is aware of the changing payment landscape, the technological advancements and consumer demands driving this change, and the policy options that have emerged as a result. The Federal Reserve is actively researching these cutting-edge technologies and collaborating closely with public and private partners in order to safeguard the long-term stability of the financial system.

Chapter Summary

– Central bank digital currencies (CBDCs) are official tender issued by a central bank in digital form. They are fiat money that is created digitally.
– CBDCs can help a central bank fulfill its mandate of providing money, preserving financial stability, and ensuring continuous access in a fully digital economy.
– CBDCs have the potential to become the most prevalent technology in the digital and transactions field.
– CBDCs would be a new form of currency issued by the government.
– CBDCs may not always be superior to other forms of payment.
– CBDCs would be safer than conventional payment methods, particularly in terms of anonymity.
– The success of CBDCs will ultimately be determined by governments, jurisdictions, and design.
– CBDCs would be treated in accounting terms akin to that of conventional fiat money.

Discussion Questions and Task
– How do you think CBDCs will impact the role of commercial banks in the payment system?
– What are the potential benefits and risks of using CBDCs for consumers and businesses?
– How do you think CBDCs will impact the stability of the financial system?
– In what ways do you think CBDCs could be used to promote financial inclusion?
– What are some of the challenges that central banks will face in issuing and managing CBDCs?
– How do you think CBDCs will affect the relationship between governments and their citizens?
– How do CBDCs compare to other forms of digital currency, such as cryptocurrencies?
– How do you think international trade and cross-border transactions will be impacted by CBDCs?
– How do you think CBDCs will impact monetary policy?
– How do you think the use of CBDCs will change over time and what impact could this have on the economy and society?

Task

XYZ Corporation has just started accepting CBDCs as a form of payment for its goods and services. On January 1, the company had $100,000 in CBDCs in its cash account. During the month of January, the company sold goods and services for $500,000 in CBDCs and incurred $50,000 in expenses related to CBDC transactions. At the end of January, the company had $450,000 in CBDCs in its cash account.

Instructions

- Using the information provided, prepare a balance sheet for XYZ Corporation as of January 31.
- Using the information provided, prepare an income statement for the month of January.
- In the notes to the financial statements, disclose any information about the company's CBDC transactions and holdings that may be material to investors and other stakeholders.

Solution notes

- Balance sheet: To prepare the balance sheet, you would need to list all of the company's assets, liabilities, and equity as of January 31. For this exercise, you would need to show the cash account with the $450,000 in CBDCs as an asset.
- Income statement: To prepare the income statement, you would need to list all of the company's revenues and expenses for the month of January. For this exercise, you would need to show the revenue of $500,000 from the sale of goods and services in CBDCs and the expenses of $50,000 related to CBDC transactions.
- Notes to the financial statements: In the notes to the financial statements, you would need to disclose any information about the company's CBDC transactions and holdings that may be material to investors and other stakeholders. For this exercise, you would need to provide information such as the total value of CBDCs held at the end of the reporting period, any changes in the value of CBDC holdings during the period, and any material risks associated with holding CBDCs and any significant restrictions on the use of CBDC.

Learn from the Web

To gain a deeper understanding of the different types of CBDCs and the latest research on the topic, you can use the resources provided by the Bank for International Settlements (BIS).

Instructions

- Go to the BIS webpage on CBDCs (https://www.bis.org/about/bisih/topics/cbdc.htm)
- Read through the introduction to CBDCs and the different types of CBDCs (e.g., retail CBDC, wholesale CBDC)
- Explore the latest research on CBDCs by clicking on the "Research & publications" tab and selecting relevant reports or articles.
- For each type of CBDC, summarize the key points and take note of any questions or areas of interest that arise.
- As a group, discuss and compare your findings and consider how CBDCs could potentially impact the economy and financial system.

References

Adrian, T. & Mancini-Griffoli, T. (2019). The Rise of Digital Money. IMF FinTech Note No. 19/01, July, pp. 2–12.

Andolfatto, D., Berentsen, A., & Martin, F. M. (2020). Money, banking, and financial markets. The Review of Economic Studies, 87(5), 2049–2086.

Assenmacher, K., Berentsen, A., Brand, C., & Lamersdorf, N. (2021). A unified framework for CBDC design: remuneration, collateral haircuts and quantity constraints.

BIS (2020). Central bank digital currencies: foundational principles and core features. [Online] Available at: https://www.bis.org/publ/othp33.pdf

Bech, M. L., Faruqui, U., Ougaard, F. & Picillo, C. (2018). Payments are a-changin' but cash still rules. *BIS Quarterly Review*, pp. 67–80.

Boar, C., Holden, H., & Wadsworth, A. (2020). Impending arrival–a sequel to the survey on central bank digital currency. BIS paper, (107).

Boar, C. & Wehrli, A., (2021). Ready, steady, go? Bank for International Settlements. Avaiable at: https://www.bis.org/publ/bppdf/bispap114.pdf

Buchholz, K. (July 21, 2022). Where Central Banks Have Issued Digital Currencies. Retrieved April 15, 2023, from https://www.statista.com/chart/24571/central-bank-digital-currencies-around-the-world/

Chiu, J., & Davoodalhosseini, S. M. (2021). *Central bank digital currency and banking: Macroeconomic benefits of a cash-like design* (No. 2021-63). Bank of Canada Staff Working Paper.

Chiu, J., & Rivadeneyra, F. (2021). An overview of the Bank of Canada CBDC project. Central Bank Digital Currency Considerations, Projects, Outlook.

Deloitte (2021). Central Bank Digital Currencies: Building Block of the Future Value Transfer [Online] Available at: https://www2.deloitte.com/content/dam/Deloitte/in/Documents/financial-services/in-fs-cbdc-noexp.pdf

Gürtler, K., Rasmussen, K., Nielsen, S. T. and Spange, M. (2017). Central Bank Digital Currency in Denmark? [Online] Available at: https://www.nationalbanken.dk/en/publications/Documents/2017/12/Analysis%20-%20Central%20bank%20digital%20currency%20in%20Denmark.pdf

Kaminska, I., (30 June, 2020). Walled gardens versus open markets in payments. *Financial Times*. FT Alphaville, pp. 4–5. Available at: https://www.ft.com/content/75ae3ae0-c09f-4242-ab3e-f293d67d5c07

Keister, T., Sanches, D., (2019). Should Central Banks Issue Digital Currency? Working Papers, No 19–26, Federal Reserve Bank of Philadelphia.

Kiff, M. J., Alwazir, J., Davidovic, S., Farias, A., Khan, M. A., Khiaonarong, M. T., & Zhou, P. (2020). A survey of research on retail central bank digital currency. [Online] Available at: https://www.imf.org/en/Publications/WP/Issues/2020/06/26/A-Survey-of-Research-on-Retail-Central-Bank-Digital-Currency-49517

Mancini-Griffoli, T., Peria, M. S. M., Agur, I., Ari, A., Kiff, J., Popescu, A., & Rochon, C. (2018). Casting light on central bank digital currency. *IMF staff discussion note*, 8(18), 1–39.

Tett, G. (5 August, 2021). How the Fed's digital currency could displace crypto. *Financial Times*. [Online] Available at: https://www.ft.com/content/14b0fc81-ac17-4436-89ac-09d71c15d2af

Further Reading

Ahnert, T., Assenmacher, K., Hoffmann, P., Leonello, A., Monet, C., & Porcellacchia, D. (2022). The economics of central bank digital currency. Available at: https://www.ecb.europa.eu/pub/pdf/scpwps/ecb.wp2713~91ddff9e7c.en.pdf

Böhme, R., Christin, N., Edelman, B., Moore, T., & Shoshitaishvili, Y. (2015). Bitcoin: Economics, Technology, and Governance. Journal of Economic Perspectives, 29(2),213–238.

Fung, B. S., & Halaburda, H. (2016). Central bank digital currencies: a framework for assessing why and how. Available at SSRN 2994052.

Prasad, E. S. (2021). *The Future of Money: How the Digital Revolution Is Transforming Currencies and Finance*. Harvard University Press.

4 Differences Between Central Bank Digital Currencies and Cryptocurrency

Key Differences Between CBDCs and Crypto

- While cryptocurrencies are decentralized and not under the control of any government or entity, central bank digital currencies (CBDCs) are issued and managed by central banks.
- While cryptocurrencies' legal status varies from nation to nation and may not be accepted as legal cash, CBDCs are recognized as legal tender and have legal standing in their respective jurisdictions.
- Compared to cryptocurrencies, which serve as a decentralized and secure form of payment and a store of value, CBDCs serve as a digital substitute for cash and are designed to increase the effectiveness of the payment system.

Introduction

The necessity to understand the distinctions between cryptocurrencies and CBDCs derives from the fact that these two types of digital currency are separate, function according to different principals, and have different effects on the economy and financial system. CBDCs are issued and backed by central banks, and the national currency serves as a direct benchmark for their worth. Their primary goal is to increase the effectiveness and security of the current payment system. They are not meant to replace actual cash or bank deposits. Regulatory oversight and anti-money laundering/counter-terrorist financing (AML/CFT) rules also apply to them.

On the other hand, cryptocurrencies are decentralized digital assets that are neither created nor backed by any one centralized organization. They utilize blockchain technology, and market demand determines their price. They are not as heavily regulated as CBDCs and are primarily used as a means of exchange, a store of value, and a form of speculation. For policymakers, regulators, financial institutions, and consumers, knowing the distinction between CBDCs and cryptocurrencies is crucial because it may help them navigate the potential risks and opportunities of digital currencies and make wise decisions.

Central Bank Digital Currency

A CBDC is a digital form of legal currency issued by a government. The central bank of a nation is responsible for issuing and administering a CBDC, which is similar to cryptocurrencies in that it utilizes a digital ledger to facilitate fast and secure digital transactions, which may or may not be based on blockchain technology. At present, the general public only has access to central bank money in the form of physical cash.

https://doi.org/10.1515/9783110982398-004

However, the implementation of CBDCs would enable faster and more secure digital payments for the general population, owing to the benefits of crypto technology.

It is worth noting that, as a CBDC lacks intrinsic financial value, the central bank may, in certain circumstances, even prohibit stockpiling or investment in one. Furthermore, research suggests that the primary purpose of digital currencies is to facilitate business-to-business transactions. Another crucial consideration is the type of blockchain cryptocurrency that CBDCs utilize. Given that central banks may, for various reasons, opt not to publicly disclose transactions and other financial data on the blockchain, a CBDC based on a private blockchain network would suffice.

This type of ledger includes permissioned blockchain networks, which store data differently than their decentralized counterparts. To access and alter the distributed ledger, members of the network (in this case the central bank) require authorization from the chain's highest authority. Financial institutions and banks collaborating with the central bank to host nodes in such a system would facilitate financial transactions, and no one outside of these entities would be able to utilize the private blockchain or perform their duties.

Cryptocurrency

Cryptocurrencies are digital assets that are globally dispersed and stored on permissioned blockchain networks. Users may acquire tokens in exchange for making contributions to the network through various techniques – the most popular of which include mining and staking. The amount of tokens may be fixed or random. A cryptocurrency blockchain network enables anyone to join and view its state, regardless of their level of involvement. Additionally, users may choose to become miners, and anyone can host a node. On a blockchain network such as the one used by Bitcoin, all users have the same rights, obligations, and level of power. The lack of noteworthy individuals among the network's users does not detract from its effectiveness, as users are in sync with the ledger's current state.

Cryptocurrencies can be classified as both currency and assets, depending on their usage. By purchasing and selling Bitcoin on exchanges and other investment platforms, speculators may participate in the fluctuations of the cryptocurrency market. Alternatively, as a hedge against rising prices and economic uncertainty, individuals may adopt innovative endeavors like Bitcoin. Furthermore, anyone can use cryptocurrency as money; anyone with a computer can use a cryptocurrency like Ethereum or Bitcoin to make a purchase or send money to someone else. Online purchases are now more straightforward than ever thanks to Bitcoin. In recent times, decentralized digital assets have been increasingly utilized to replace traditional forms of internet money.

CBDC vs. Cryptocurrency

It is essential to understand that CBDCs are not the same as decentralized cryptocurrencies. Unlike cryptocurrencies, CBDCs are entirely controlled by a single entity. This means that users of a cryptocurrency have complete autonomy over their financial activity, in contrast to CBDC users.

In the United States, for example, the assets of the CBDC will be issued and stored in a centralized location. CBDCs can be thought of as the digital version of traditional money, such as the dollar or rupiah. This means that your identification and transaction data will be linked to your CBDC holdings, and the details of a transaction will only be visible to the recipient, the sender, and the bank. This sets CBDCs apart from other cryptocurrencies, as it is well known that anyone can view the transaction data on a cryptocurrency network, but this information cannot be used to identify the user. Below, we will explore some further significant differences between cryptocurrency and CBDCs.

Conceptual Differences

We present the conceptual differences between CBDC and cryptocurrency below:

Openness

CBDCs, which are employed by central banks around the world, are viewed as a means to enhance the existing fiat monetary system. The establishment of a varied monetary landscape hinges on the technical capabilities of cryptocurrencies, underpinned by a central bank's underlying trust.

The CBDC ecosystem is composed of the central bank, commercial banks, and final consumers. The central bank controls the creation, redemption, and circulation of coins. Commercial banks act as intermediaries between customers and central banks. Customers have the option of making instantaneous payments and new agreements. Customers can range from sole proprietorships to global enterprises, and payments can be made locally, nationally, or internationally.

Although there are instances in which cryptocurrencies do offer a degree of anonymity, no one can make the claim that they are completely anonymous. It is important to note that while some individuals claim that certain cryptocurrencies are completely anonymous, any assertion of completely anonymous transactions needs to be approached with caution.

Permissibility

It is important to note that CBDCs are not without risks. If individuals and companies sought to withdraw money from traditional bank accounts by converting to CBDCs during a financial crisis, it could accelerate a bank run. Consequently, the control of the entire supply of CBDCs is vital. Furthermore, it is important to distinguish between different types of digital currencies.

Scalability

Scalability, long identified as a significant challenge for the development of digital currencies, is a result of the decentralized system in which there is no central authority and everyone is responsible for maintaining the stability of the currency. A large, complex system that is difficult for most users to verify is preferred over a small, simple system that is easy to check. The creation of widely accepted and easily verifiable digital money has made significant progress, with the MIT Digital Currency Initiative (DCI) playing a pivotal role. Researchers at the DCI are working on various projects, such as the Lightning Network, Utreexo, SpaceMint, and Discreet Log Contracts, to expand the capabilities of digital money.

Due to its decentralized structure, Bitcoin has emerged as the most successful cryptocurrency to date. The underlying protocol – the Nakamoto Consensus – requires proof of work, which has the drawback of consuming a significant amount of energy. Additionally, the mining of Bitcoin has become increasingly consolidated.

SpaceMint, a cryptocurrency, relies on proofs of space rather than proofs of effort, to circumvent these issues. In SpaceMint, disk space is more crucial than processing power for miners. We argue that several issues faced by Bitcoin, such as excessive energy consumption, are eliminated or significantly reduced through the design of SpaceMint. Additionally, SpaceMint fairly rewards miners of all sizes for their contributions to the network.

Decentralization

The notion of digitizing fiat money began to gain significant attention among researchers and central banks worldwide following the surge in popularity of Bitcoin in 2017. The aim of this interest is to fully utilize the advantages offered by digital technology in order to maintain the competitiveness of fiat currencies (Bordo and Levin 2017). The speed and cost-efficiency of Bitcoin transfers, compared to other methods used for handling cross-border payments, highlighted the limitations of traditional paper money.

There is potential for further research to be conducted on the advantages of digital systems when compared to CBDCs that are kept in a single place. If the system is well administered as a whole, it has the capacity to provide free and stable international liquidity to all member countries across the world, eliminating the need for countries to borrow money or purchase foreign currency in order to meet their foreign exchange reserve requirements. This can potentially bring financial stability back to the balance sheets of participating countries, and permanently resolve global imbalances. Additionally, by stabilizing exchange rates and reducing imbalances, this approach has the potential to enhance the international monetary system, without the need for economic integration. It can be implemented globally, and promotes participation from any nation.

Application Scenarios

CBDCs present several advantages in both domestic and international payment scenarios. For domestic payments, CBDCs can facilitate efficient and cost-effective transactions between customers, businesses, and individuals within the country's borders. Furthermore, CBDCs also prove to be highly beneficial in the context of international transfers, particularly in the realm of global trade, where cross-border payments are a common occurrence.

Design Requirements

CBDCs have the potential to enhance accessibility as both a medium of exchange and a form of digital fiat currency. CBDC payments should be swift, cost-effective, and secure, much like traditional fiat money (cash). Features of a well-designed CBDC should include offline and instantaneous payments, privacy and anonymity, security, resilience, controlled regulation, availability, scalability, simplicity, and user-friendliness.

In addition to online and instantaneous cash transactions, CBDCs should also facilitate offline and prompt cash transactions. The term "dual offline" refers to a transaction in which neither party is connected to the internet. Furthermore, all financial transactions should be promptly addressed and completed. Anonymity and privacy are of paramount importance. For end users to feel secure when using CBDCs and completing transactions, it is essential that their identities and transactions remain anonymous.

Security is of paramount importance in the digital realm, and thus privacy and security are essential for CBDCs. Essential security features to fend off fraud and other dangers include measures to prevent double-spending, anti-counterfeiting, non-repudiation, and verifiability. This means that if a CBDC has already been used in one transaction, it cannot be used in another. To safeguard users' funds from counterfeiting, CBDCs must incorporate anti-counterfeiting measures. All CBDC-related acts must be recorded and reversible in order to be non-repudiable. For a transaction to be considered verifiable, it must be possible for a third party to verify it.

Resilience is also essential, as the CBDC system must be able to recover from any foreseeable failures. It needs to be fault tolerant. Additionally, the ability for CBDCs to be controlled and regulated is crucial, as they are required to comply with all relevant laws. Availability is also important, as the CBDC must be able to manage payments every day of the year. Scalability is also crucial, as the CBDC must be flexible enough to handle an increase in transaction volume without incurring additional costs. Finally, ease of use is paramount, as everyone, even those without telephones, should be able to utilize CBDCs with ease. It is possible that central banks will provide the technology required for offline transactions. We present a summary of these conceptual differences in Table 4.1.

Table 4.1: Differences between CBDCs and cryptocurrency.

CHARACTERISTICS	CBDC	CRYPTOCURRENCY
OPENNESS	Not at all anonymous.	Mostly anonymous, making it difficult to track down its original owners. Open to a variety of investors. The Colonial Pipeline hack shows how easy it is to track down Bitcoin transactions once transactions are made.
PERMISSIBILITY	For something to be considered real CBDC, it must be issued as a central bank liability. This is how private money, such as credit balances on accounts in commercial banks, differs from central bank money.	It is not a legally binding tender. Prices are independent of any underlying economic value, even if they are frequently exchanged and speculated on.
SPEED	The CBDC program of the United States has achieved significant strides. The digital dollar surpassed even the most advanced cryptocurrency networks, setting a new transaction record of 1.7 million through its transaction processing system (TPS).	The biggest cryptocurrencies with the greatest transaction speeds include Solana (a public blockchain platform), with 50,000 TPS, and Algorand, with 1,000 TPS. The two best-known blockchains, Bitcoin or Ethereum, have transaction throughputs of only 34 and 10 TPS, respectively.

Table 4.1 (continued)

CHARACTERISTICS	CBDC	CRYPTOCURRENCY
SCALABILITY	Centralized and dependent on a central bank. Scalability has long been recognized as a major barrier to the development of digital currencies. In a decentralized system without a central authority, everyone is equally responsible for preserving the stability of the currency. A large, difficult-for-most users-to-verify system wins over a small, straightforward-to-check system.	Due to its decentralized structure, Bitcoin has become the most successful cryptocurrency ever developed. The underlying protocol (the Nakamoto Consensus) requires proof of work in order to do this, which has the drawback of costing a significant amount of energy. The various Bitcoin mining technologies have also been steadily consolidated.
DECENTRALIZATION	All privileges in the digital system are available to CBDCs. Global financial transfers and transactions may be completed quickly and at no cost using the organic system.	While decentralization has pros and cons, the former clearly outweigh the latter. Decentralization is cryptocurrency's most salient and distinctive feature, even though it may ultimately endanger its reliability and viability.

Operation Differences

We present the operational differences between CBDC and cryptocurrency below:

Central Bank Digital Currency

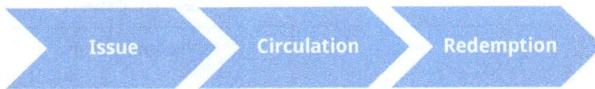

Figure 4.1: Operational structure of a CBDC.

A CBDC operates based on three mechanisms: issue, circulation, and redemption (as depicted in Figure 4.1):
- Issue: A central bank issues a CBDC to commercial banks and other forms of financial institutions. This process is similar to how a central bank issues actual monetary currency to the economy.
- Circulation: CBDCs can be used for a wide range of transactions due to the similarity to fiat currency. Users of CBDCs include individuals, companies, and other organizations. One difference between the issue of fiat currency and a CBDC is

that the central bank needs to maintain a distributed ledger on which CBDC transactions are recorded.
– Redemption: Commercial banks and other financial organizations may exchange CBDCs for current forms of currency, such as cash or reserves.

Cryptocurrencies

Blockchain technology, a type of decentralized technology, is the foundation of the cryptocurrency operating model. Transactions are recorded on a public ledger that is kept up to date by a network of nodes, and it runs on a peer-to-peer network. These nodes carry out transaction processing and validation before adding them to the blockchain.

Transaction processing and validation are done through mining. To verify transactions and add new blocks to the blockchain, miners utilize specialized hardware and software to solve challenging mathematical equations. They are compensated with cryptocurrencies in return.

Digital wallets, which are software programs that let users examine their balances, conduct transactions, and keep track of their past transactions, let users store and manage their cryptocurrency. Users can also trade cryptocurrency on decentralized exchanges, which are platforms that allow users to buy and sell cryptocurrency directly with other users, without the need for a centralized intermediary. We present a summary of these operational differences in Table 4.2.

Table 4.2: Difference in accounting practices between CBDCs and cryptocurrency.

Feature	CBDC	Cryptocurrency
Entity	Central bank	Independent issuer
Recording Process	Centralized ledger	Decentralized ledger
Transparency	High	Moderate
Reporting Requirements	Traditional financial reporting	Reporting requirements varies across jurisdiction
Auditing	Auditable by financial institutions and regulators	Difficult to perform audit
Accounting Standards	Follows Generally Accepted Accounting Principles (GAAP) and International Financial Reporting Standards	Does not follow any specific accounting standards

Chapter Summary

- For policymakers, regulators, financial institutions, and consumers, knowing the difference between cryptocurrencies and central bank digital currencies (CBDCs) is crucial.
- CBDCs are issued and backed by central banks, while cryptocurrencies are decentralized digital assets that are neither created nor backed by any one centralized organization.
- A CBDC is a digital form of legal currency issued by the government.
- Central banks may, for various reasons, opt not to publicly disclose transactions and other financial data on the blockchain.
- Research suggests that the primary purpose of digital currencies is to facilitate business-to-business transactions.
- Cryptocurrencies are digital assets that are stored on permissioned blockchain networks.
- CBDCs are not the same as decentralized cryptocurrencies. Unlike cryptocurrencies, CBDCs are entirely controlled by a single entity.
- The establishment of a diverse monetary environment is dependent on the technical potential of cryptocurrencies, supported by the underlying trust of central banks.
- The CBDC ecosystem comprises central banks, commercial banks, and end consumers. A study found that cryptocurrencies are superior to fiat currencies in achieving the objectives of a future monetary system.

Discussion Questions
- What are the main variations in issuance, control, and regulation between a CBDC and a cryptocurrency?
- What distinguishes a CBDC's architecture and underlying technology from a cryptocurrency?
- How do decentralized cryptocurrency networks' monetary goals and practices compare to those of central banks?
- From the viewpoints of governments, central banks, and consumers, what potential advantages and hazards are connected with the introduction of CBDCs and cryptocurrencies?
- What effects might the rising use of cryptocurrencies and CBDCs have on the established banking system and financial intermediaries?
- How do characteristics like security, privacy, and scalability differ between CBDCs and cryptocurrencies?
- What effects will cryptocurrencies and CBDCs have on monetary policy and financial stability?
- How do the accounting practices of CBDCs and cryptocurrency differ?
- How do the legal and regulatory frameworks surrounding CBDCs and cryptocurrency differ?
- What are the potential future developments and trends in CBDCs and cryptocurrency?

Learn from the Web
The following resources provide more insight on the difference between CBDCs and cryptocurrency:
- The Bank for International Settlements (BIS): https://www.bis.org/about/bisih/topics/cbdc.htm
- The International Monetary Fund (IMF): https://www.imf.org/en/Publications/fandd/issues/2022/09/Picture-this-The-ascent-of-CBDCs
- The European Central Bank (ECB): https://www.ecb.europa.eu/home/search/html/central_bank_digital_currencies_cbdc.en.html
- The World Economic Forum (WEF): https://www.weforum.org/agenda/2023/01/davos23-central-bank-digital-currency-redesigning-money
- The World Bank: https://openknowledge.worldbank.org/handle/10986/36765

References

Areddy, J. T. (5 April, 2021). China Creates Its Own Digital Currency, a First for Major Economy. *The Wall Street Journal*. [Online] Available at: https://www.wsj.com/articles/china-creates-its-own-digital-currency-a-first-for-major-economy-11617634118#:~:text=China's%20version%20of%20a%20digital, draws%3A%20anonymity%20for%20the%20user.

Bordo, M. D., & Levin, A. T. (2017). Central Bank Digital Currency and the Future of Monetary Policy. NBER Working Paper. Cambridge: NBER. doi:10.3386/W23711. [Online] Available at: https://www.nber.org/system/files/working_papers/w23711/w23711.pdf

Further Reading

Davoodalhosseini, S. M. (2022). Central bank digital currency and monetary policy. *Journal of Economic Dynamics and Control, 142*, 104150.

Morgan, J. (2022). Systemic stablecoin and the defensive case for Central Bank Digital Currency: A critique of the Bank of England's framing. *Research in International Business and Finance, 62*, 101716.

Ozili, P. K. (2022). Circular Economy and Central Bank Digital Currency. *Circular Economy and Sustainability, 2*, 1501–1516.

Soderberg, G., Bechara, M. M., Bossu, W., Che, M. N. X., Davidovic, S., Kiff, M. J., & Yoshinaga, A. (2022). Behind the Scenes of Central Bank Digital Currency: Emerging Trends, Insights, and Policy Lessons. Available at:https://www.elibrary.imf.org/view/journals/063/2022/004/article-A001-en.xml

5 Central Bank Digital Currencies Around the World

Introduction

Digital renditions of fiat money that are produced and supported by central banks are known as central bank digital currencies (CBDCs). They are currently being created and used all over the world as central banks investigate the potential advantages and difficulties of releasing digital currencies. CBDCs have the potential to boost financial inclusion, increase payment system efficiency and security, and open up new monetary policy opportunities. However, there are also worries about the potential risks and difficulties, such as the impact on monetary policy, privacy, and financial stability. While the United States and some nations in the European Union are still in the research and development stage, others, like China and Sweden, have already started their own CBDC pilot programs. The exact form and functionality of CBDCs may vary across countries, but they all aim to provide a secure and efficient digital alternative to cash. We list the CBDCs around the world (at various stages of development) in Table 5.1 and the summary in Figure 5.1

Sand Dollar: The Central Bank of the Bahamas' Digital Currency

As a result of Project Sand Dollar in December 2019, the Central Bank of the Bahamas (CBOB) introduced the Sand Dollar, a digital version of the Bahamian dollar. The primary objective of this initiative was to improve financial inclusion, access, and the efficiency and competitiveness of the domestic payment system.

The CBOB justified the introduction of the Sand Dollar by referencing the Bahamas Financial Literacy Results of 2018, which revealed that only 48% of individuals

https://doi.org/10.1515/9783110982398-005

Table 5.1: CBDCs around the world.

No.	Digital Currency	Country/Region	Central Bank(s)	Year	Status
1	Sand Dollar	Bahamas	Central Bank of the Bahamas	2022	Launched
2	JAM-DEX	Jamaica	Bank of Jamaica	2022	Launched
3	eNaira	Nigeria	Central Bank of Nigeria	2022	Launched
4	DCash	Eastern Caribbean Economic and Currency Union	Eastern Caribbean Central Bank	2022	Launched
5	Wholesale CBDC	France	Banque de France	2022	Pilot
6	Project Ubin	Singapore	Monetary Authority of Singapore	2022	Pilot
7	Digital rupee	India	Reserve Bank of India	2022	Pilot
8	e-CNY	China	People's Bank of China	2022	Pilot
9	e-Cedi	Ghana	Bank of Ghana	2021	Pilot
10	France and Tunisia CBDC	France and Tunisia	Banque de France and Banque Centrale de Tunisie	2021	Pilot
11	France and Singapore CBDC	France and Singapore	Banque de France and the Monetary Authority of Singapore (MAS)	2021	Pilot
12	Project Aber	Saudi Arabia and United Arab Emirates	Saudi Central Bank and Central Bank of the UAE	2019	Pilot
13	Project Jasper	Canada	Bank of Canada	2016	Pilot
14	e-Peso	Uruguay	Central Bank of Uruguay	2014	Pilot
15	e-krona	Sweden	Sveriges Riksbank	2022	Proof of concept
16	Digital tenge	Kazakhstan	National Bank of Kazakhstan	2022	Proof of concept
17	Digital yen	Japan	Bank of Japan	2022	Proof of concept
18	Digital real	Brazil	Central Bank of Brazil	2022	Proof of concept
19	Digital lira	Turkey	Central Bank of the Republic of Turkey	2022	Proof of concept

Table 5.1 (continued)

No.	Digital Currency	Country/Region	Central Bank(s)	Year	Status
20	Digital won	South Korea	Bank of Korea	2022	Proof of concept
21	Digital ruble	Russian Federation	Bank of Russia	2022	Proof of concept
22	Norway CBDC	Norway	Norges Bank	2022	Proof of concept
23	Crypto rial	Iran	Central Bank of Iran	2022	Proof of concept
24	Thailand CBDC	Thailand	Bank of Thailand	2022	Proof of concept
25	Hungary CBDC	Hungary	Hungarian National Bank	2022	Proof of concept
26	New Zealand CBDC	New Zealand	Reserve Bank of New Zealand	2022	Proof of concept
27	e-ringgit	Malaysia	Central Bank of Malaysia	2022	Proof of concept
28	Taiwan CBDC	Taiwan	Central Bank of Taiwan	2020	Proof of concept
29	South Korea CBDC	South Korea	Bank of Korea	2020	Proof of concept
30	Project Inthanon-LionRock	Hong Kong	Hong Kong Monetary Authority	2019	Proof of concept
31	e-shekel	Israel	Bank of Israel	2017	Proof of concept
32	e-hryvnia	Ukraine	National Bank of Ukraine	2017	Proof of concept
33	Sweden CBDC	Sweden	Sveriges Riksbank		Proof of concept
35	Spain CBDC	Spain	Banco de España	2022	Research
36	CBDCPH	Philippines	Bangko Sentral ng Pilipinas	2022	Research
37	Pakistan CBDC	Pakistan	State Bank of Pakistan	2022	Research

Table 5.1 (continued)

No.	Digital Currency	Country/Region	Central Bank(s)	Year	Status
38	Mongolia CBDC	Mongolia	Bank of Mongolia	2022	Research
39	Digital GEL	Georgia	National Bank of Georgia	2022	Research
40	eAUD	Australia	Reserve Bank of Australia	2022	Research
41	Retail digital euro	Euro area	European Central Bank	2022	Research
42	e-dollar	Canada	Bank of Canada	2022	Research
43	mBridge	Hong Kong, Thailand, China, and UAE	Hong Kong Monetary Authority, Bank of Thailand, People's Bank of China, and Central Bank of the United Arab Emirates	2022	Research
44	Sri Lanka CBDC	Sri Lanka	Central Bank of Sri Lanka	2022	Research
45	Nepal CBDC	Nepal	Nepal Rastra Bank	2022	Research
46	Namibia CBDC	Namibia	Bank of Namibia	2022	Research
47	Laos CBDC	Laos	Bank of the Lao PDR	2022	Research
48	CBDC Israel, Norway and Sweden	Israel, Norway and Sweden	Bank of Israel, Norges Bank, and Sveriges Riksbank	2022	Research
49	Wholesale digital euro	Euro area	European Central Bank	2022	Research
50	e-lilangeni	Eswatini	Central Bank of Eswatini	2022	Research
51	United States of America CBDC	United States of America	US Federal Reserve	2022	Research
52	India CBDC	India	Reserve Bank of India	2022	Research
53	Zimbabwe CBDC	Zimbabwe	Reserve Bank of Zimbabwe	2022	Research
54	Digital rupiah	Indonesia	Bank Indonesia	2022	Research
55	Mauritius CBDC	Mauritius	Bank of Mauritius	2022	Research
56	India CBDC	India	Reserve Bank of India	2022	Research

Table 5.1 (continued)

No.	Digital Currency	Country/Region	Central Bank(s)	Year	Status
57	Project Sela	Israel, Hong Kong	The BIS Innovation Hub, the Bank of Israel, and the Hong Kong Monetary Authority	2022	Research
58	Fiji CBDC	Fiji	Reserve Bank of Fiji	2022	Research
59	Bangladesh CBDC	Bangladesh	Bangladesh Bank	2022	Research
60	Azerbaijan CBDC	Azerbaijan	Central Bank of Azerbaijan	2022	Research
61	Sudan CBDC	Sudan	Central Bank of Sudan	2022	Research
62	Khokha	South Africa	South African Reserve Bank	2022	Research
63	Argentina CBDC	Argentina	Central Bank of Argentina	2022	Research
64	Curacao CBDC	Curacao	Central Bank of Curaçao and Sint Maarten	2022	Research
65	Trinidad and Tobago CBDC	Trinidad and Tobago	Central Bank of Trinidad and Tobago	2022	Research
66	Rwanda CBDC	Rwanda	National Bank of Rwanda	2022	Research
67	Malaysia CBDC	Malaysia	Bank Negara Malaysia	2022	Research
68	Honduras CBDC	Honduras	Central Bank of Honduras	2022	Research
69	Zambia CBDC	Zambia	Bank of Zambia	2022	Research
70	Yemen CBDC	Yemen	Central Bank of Yemen	2022	Research
71	Uganda CBDC	Uganda	Bank of Uganda	2022	Research
72	Saudi Arabia CBDC	Saudi Arabia	Saudi Arabian Central Bank	2022	Research
73	Qatar CBDC	Qatar	Qatar Central Bank	2022	Research
74	Oman CBDC	Oman	Central Bank of Oman	2022	Research
75	Iraq CBDC	Iraq	Central Bank of Iraq	2022	Research
76	Denmark CBDC	Denmark	Danmarks Nationalbank	2022	Research
77	Jordan CBDC	Jordan	Central Bank of Jordan	2022	Research

Table 5.1 (continued)

No.	Digital Currency	Country/Region	Central Bank(s)	Year	Status
78	Solomon Islands CBDC	Solomon Islands	Central Bank of Solomon Islands	2022	Research
79	Republic of Palau CBDC	Republic of Palau Bank		2021	Research
80	Hong Kong CBDC	Hong Kong	Hong Kong Monetary Authority	2021	Research
81	Mexico CBDC	Mexico	Banco de México	2021	Research
82	Tanzania CBDC	Tanzania	Bank of Tanzania	2021	Research
83	Peru CBDC	Peru	Central Reserve Bank of Peru	2021	Research
84	iQuetzal	Guatemala	Bank of Guatemala	2021	Research
85	Digital ngultrum	Bhutan	Royal Monetary Authority of Bhutan	2021	Research
86	e-Ariary	Madagascar	Central Bank of Madagascar	2021	Research
87	Vanuatu CBDC	Vanuatu	Reserve Bank of Vanuatu	2021	Research
88	Tonga CBDC	Tonga	National Reserve Bank of Tonga	2021	Research
89	Hong Kong CBDC	Hong Kong	Hong Kong Monetary Authority	2021	Research
90	Jura	France and Switzerland	Swiss National Bank, Banque de France, and the BIS	2021	Research
91	DELPHI	Austria	Austrian National Bank	2021	Research
92	South Africa CBDC	South Africa	South African Reserve Bank	2021	Research
93	Macau CBDC	Macau	Macau Government	2021	Research
94	Project Hamilton	United States of America	US Federal Reserve	2021	Research
95	Morocco CBDC	Morocco	Bank-Al-Maghrib	2021	Research
96	Czech Republic CBDC	Czech Republic	Czech National Bank	2021	Research

Table 5.1 (continued)

No.	Digital Currency	Country/Region	Central Bank(s)	Year	Status
97	Project Atom	Australia	Reserve Bank of Australia	2021	Research
98	Gourde Digitale	Haiti	Bank of the Republic of Haiti	2020	Research
99	Project Helvetia	Switzerland	Swiss National Bank	2020	Research
100	Lebanon CBDC	Lebanon	Lebanon's central bank	2020	Research
101	Digital euro	Euro area	European Central Bank	2020	Research
102	United States of America CBDC	United States of America	US Federal Reserve	2020	Research
103	Chile CBDC	Chile	Central Bank of Chile	2019	Research
104	Pakistan CBDC	Pakistan	State Bank of Pakistan	2019	Research
105	e-franc	Switzerland	Swiss National Bank	2019	Research
106	e-dinar	Tunisia	Central Bank of Tunisia	2019	Research
107	Kuwait CBDC	Kuwait	Central Bank of Kuwait	2019	Research
108	Kenya CBDC	Kenya	Central Bank of Kenya	2018	Research
109	Egypt CBDC	Egypt	Central Bank of Egypt	2018	Research
110	United Kingdom CBDC	United Kingdom	Bank of England	2018	Research
111	Digital rial	Iran	Central Bank of Iran	2018	Research
112	Rafkrona	Iceland	Central Bank of Iceland	2018	Research
113	Palestine CBDC	Palestine	Palestine Monetary Authority	2017	Research
114	Digital zloty	Poland	Narodowy Bank Polski	2017	Research
115	Stella	Japan	Bank of Japan	2016	Research
116	RSCoin	United Kingdom	Bank of England	2015	Research
117	Jura	Switzerland	Swiss National Bank		Research

Table 5.1 (continued)

No.	Digital Currency	Country/Region	Central Bank(s)	Year	Status
118	Vietnam CBDC	Vietnam	State Bank of Vietnam		Research
119	United Arab Emirates CBDC	United Arab Emirates	Central Bank of the United Arab Emirates		Research
120	Austria CBDC	Austria	Austrian National Bank		Research
121	Project Orchid	Singapore	Monetary Authority of Singapore	2022	Cancelled
122	Philippines CBDC	Philippines	Bangko Sentral ng Pilipinas	2021	Cancelled
123	Haiti CBDC	Haiti	Bank of the Republic of Haiti	2019	Cancelled
124	e-kroner	Denmark	Danmarks Nationalbank	2017	Cancelled
125	Dinero electronico	Ecuador	Central Bank of Ecuador	2017	Cancelled
126	Avant	Finland	Bank of Finland	1993	Cancelled

Source: CBDC Tracker (2023)

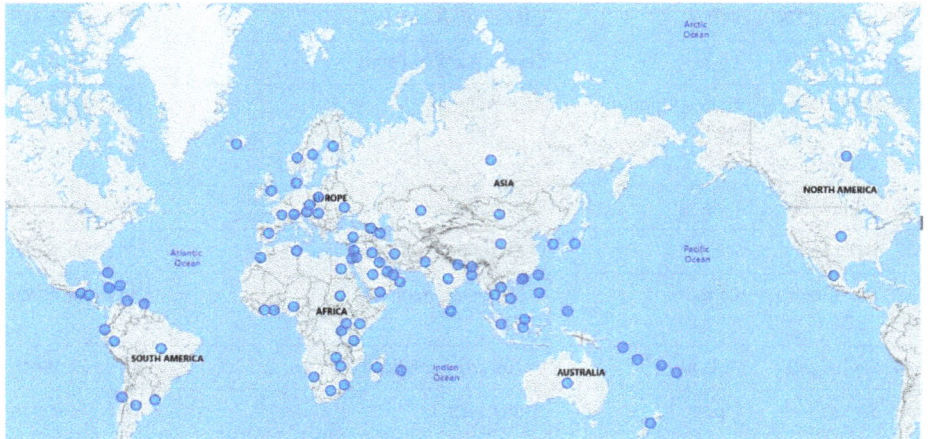

Figure 5.1: CBDCs around the world.
Source: CBDC Tracker (2023)

had access to credit card facilities from the traditional banking sector. Additionally, the CBOB acknowledged the difficulties that arose from strict customer due diligence and "know your customer" requirements in accessing traditional banking services. Therefore, the CBOB identified the need to modernize the payment system and sought to leverage digital payment infrastructure. Figure 5.2 provides a historical overview of the development of the Sand Dollar.

The Sand Dollar plays a crucial role in the payment system modernization initiative implemented by the CBOB. The CBOB expects that the Sand Dollar will enable it to achieve universal access to digital payments and financial services, support government efforts to digitalize the financial system, and facilitate efficient spending and tax administration.

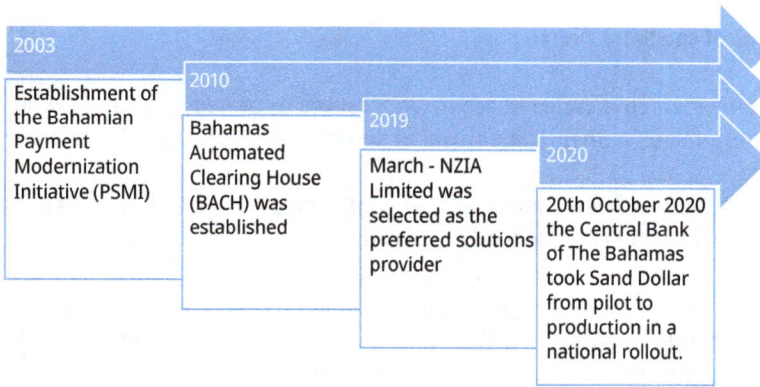

2003
Establishment of the Bahamian Payment Modernization Initiative (PSMI)

2010
Bahamas Automated Clearing House (BACH) was established

2019
March - NZIA Limited was selected as the preferred solutions provider

2020
20th October 2020 the Central Bank of The Bahamas took Sand Dollar from pilot to production in a national rollout.

Figure 5.2: Historical overview of the Sand Dollar.
Source: Central Bank of the Bahamas (2019)

Key Players in the Creation of Sand Dollar

The stakeholders of the Sand Dollar, introduced in December 2019, can be broadly categorized into primary and secondary groups.

– Primary stakeholders of the Sand Dollar include the CBOB, the public sector, and entities other than licensed financial intermediaries. These stakeholders are directly involved in the development and implementation of the Sand Dollar initiative.

– Secondary stakeholders of the Sand Dollar include the general public and analysts. These stakeholders are not directly involved in the initiative but may be affected by its outcomes.

The successful development and launch of the Sand Dollar was the result of contributions from various key players, including:

- Project sponsors: The CBOB serves as the project sponsor and plays the role of both issuing and monitoring the Sand Dollar.
- Financial partners: Clearing banks, credit unions, money transmission businesses, and payment service providers serve as key financial intermediaries in the real-world application of the Sand Dollar. Examples of financial partners include SunCash, MoneyMaxx, and Kanoo.
- Strategic partners: The government and the National Insurance Board serve as strategic partners, as the two largest originators of digital payments in the Bahamas.
- Technology partners: Technology partners such as NZIA and Avertium have been instrumental in ensuring the transactional efficiency and low delivery cost of the CBDC.

Security Features of the Sand Dollar

The CBOB has implemented a range of security measures to protect the Sand Dollar. These include multi-factor authentication, wallet security, and regular cybersecurity assessments.
- Multi-factor authentication is mandatory for configuring a Sand Dollar wallet, requiring users to provide two randomly generated passcodes to perform financial transactions.
- Wallet security is ensured through unique data encryption, which ensures privacy and confidentiality. Users are able to track their transactions and the ability of back-office operators to view transaction details is limited.

To ensure compliance with international standards, regular cybersecurity assessments must be conducted by all financial institutions offering a Sand Dollar wallet. These assessments review the overall cybersecurity of the financial institution, including its mobile app.

Types of Sand Dollar

There are two types of Sand Dollar available for a diverse range of customers.
- Business: This type of wallet is available for commercial users. Proof of regulated status is required to access the commercial Sand Dollar wallet. Business e-wallets have a holding limit between $8,000 and $1 million.
- Personal: There are two types of personal Sand Dollar wallets:
  - Individual I is for unbanked, non-residents and visitors. It has a wallet-holding limit of $500.
  - Individual II has a high wallet ceiling of up to $8,000.

JAM-DEX: The Bank of Jamaica's Digital Currency

The Bank of Jamaica, the nation's central bank, developed and is the backer of Jamaica's CBDC, JAM-DEX, an electronic representation of the Jamaican dollar. JAM-DEX is intended to be a safe and effective method of payment that may be utilized for smaller, more routine financial transactions as well as for bigger, more intricate ones.

Jamaica's pursuit of a CBDC is motivated by a number of factors. First and foremost, it is seen as a means of enhancing the effectiveness and speed of payments, particularly for individuals who do not have access to conventional financial services. Jamaicans will be able to use their mobile phones and other devices to send and receive payments immediately and around the clock thanks to the CBDC. A CBDC is also thought to be able to lessen the quantity of currency in circulation, which may be expensive to generate and carry and is also susceptible to theft and forgery.

The Bank of Jamaica will issue and support Jamaica's CBDC, which will be legal tender much like actual money. A digital wallet accessible via a mobile phone or other device will be used to build the CBDC utilizing blockchain technology. The CBDC will be built to be extremely secure, and it will employ cutting-edge technology for authentication and encryption to guard against fraud and cyberattacks.

Like actual currency, JAM-DEX will be accepted by retailers and other companies. It may also be used for internet purchases. The issuance and distribution will be supervised by the Bank of Jamaica. Jamaica's JAM-DEX is a decentralized exchange built on the Algorand blockchain. The project is still in development, we present a rough timeline of key events and milestones in Table 5.2.

Table 5.2: Key events and milestones for JAM-DEX.

August 2020	The Jamaica Stock Exchange (JSE) announces that it will be developing a digital asset trading platform called the Jamaican Digital Exchange (JAM-DEX). The platform will be built on the Algorand blockchain, a high-speed, low-cost blockchain designed for decentralized finance (DeFi) applications.
October 2020	The JSE signs a memorandum of understanding (MOU) with Algorand to help develop the JAM-DEX platform.
December 2020	The JSE launches a pilot program for the JAM-DEX platform, allowing selected market participants to test the platform and provide feedback.
April 2021	The JSE announces that it has received regulatory approval to launch the JAM-DEX platform. The platform is scheduled to go live in Q3 2021.
July 2021	The JSE announces that it has partnered with blockchain company Blockstation to provide the technology for the JAM-DEX platform.

Table 5.2 (continued)

August 2021	The JSE announces that it has completed the onboarding of broker-dealers onto the JAM-DEX platform. The platform is still being tested but is expected to go live in the coming weeks.
October 2021	The JSE announces that the JAM-DEX platform is now live and open to the public. The platform currently supports trading in Bitcoin, Ether, and the Jamaican dollar-backed stablecoin.
May 2022	The Bank of Jamaica is pleased to advise that the phased rollout of JAM-DEX has progressed with the amendments to the Bank of Jamaica Act (BOJA) 2020 being passed into law on 14th June 2022.

Source: Central Bank of Jamaica (2023)

The Jamaica Stock Exchange's (JSE) decentralized exchange, JAM-DEX, is based on the Algorand blockchain, a fast, affordable blockchain made for decentralized finance (DeFi) applications. A permissionless, pure proof-of-stake blockchain called Algorand offers quick confirmation times for transactions as well as high levels of security.

Pure proof of stake (PPoS), the consensus algorithm used by the Algorand blockchain, enables anybody who owns the network's native coin, ALGO, to take part in the consensus process and earn rewards for transaction verification. In contrast, Bitcoin's proof-of-work (PoW) consensus forces miners to solve challenging mathematical puzzles in order to get rewards.

The Algorand blockchain's high transaction throughput, which supports thousands of transactions per second with little delay, is one of its distinguishing characteristics. This makes it suitable for use in DeFi applications, where quick confirmation times for transactions are essential. JAM-DEX leverages smart contracts in addition to the Algorand blockchain to make it easier to trade digital assets. Smart contracts are automatically enforcing contracts that do not require the involvement of middlemen like banks or brokers. Overall, JAM-DEX offers a quick, safe, and decentralized platform for trading digital assets thanks to the Algorand blockchain and smart contracts.

DCash: The Eastern Caribbean Central Bank's Digital Currency

The Eastern Caribbean Central Bank (ECCB) has introduced a CBDC called DCash. The Eastern Caribbean Currency Union (ECCU), which is made up of Anguilla, Antigua and Barbuda, Dominica, Grenada, Montserrat, Saint Kitts and Nevis, Saint Lucia, and Saint Vincent and the Grenadines, is governed by the ECCB as its monetary authority. In order to offer a digital representation of the Eastern Caribbean dollar (XCD), the ECCU's official currency, DCash, was introduced in March 2021 as a pilot project. The project's objective is to offer residents and companies in the area a quick, easy, and secure method to make payments and handle financial transactions.

DCash is based on blockchain technology, a decentralized ledger that makes record-keeping safe, open, and impenetrable. The Corda blockchain platform, created by R3, a top supplier of blockchain solutions, provides the foundation for the technology behind DCash. The DCash system is made to function with a variety of gadgets, such as PCs, tablets, and smartphones. On their device, users may download the DCash app and connect it to their ECCB account. Once linked, they may use DCash to send money to other users locally and abroad to make payments.

The value of DCash is tied to the Eastern Caribbean dollar since it is intended to be a stablecoin. This guarantees the stability of DCash's value and lessens the possibility of price fluctuation, which is frequently linked to other cryptocurrencies. Moreover, DCash is intended to be completely backed by the ECCB, making it fully redeemable for actual Eastern Caribbean dollars at any moment. Key events of DCash's development are presented in Table 5.3 below:

Table 5.3: Key events of DCash's development.

March 2019	The ECCB announced that it had partnered with blockchain firm Bitt to develop a digital currency for use in the Eastern Caribbean Currency Union (ECCU), which comprises eight countries in the Caribbean.
March 2020	The ECCB launched a pilot program for DCash with a small group of users testing the digital currency for transactions in the ECCU.
September 2020	The ECCB announced that it had partnered with Caribbean digital payment provider Fincross to launch a DCash wallet that would be available to users in the ECCU. The wallet would allow users to store DCash and use it to make transactions with merchants and other users in the region.
February 2021	The ECCB announced that it had completed the pilot program for DCash and that it was preparing to launch the digital currency to the public in the ECCU.
March 2021	DCash was officially launched, becoming the world's first digital currency issued by a central bank to be used as legal tender. The launch was accompanied by a public education campaign to help users understand how to use DCash and the benefits of digital currency.
August 2021	The ECCB announced that it had signed an agreement with the Barbados-based FinTech company Bitt Inc. to provide support for the continued development and expansion of DCash. The partnership includes collaboration on the development of a regional payment system and the establishment of a DCash payment gateway.

Source: East Caribbean Central Bank (2021)

eNaira: The Central Bank of Nigeria's Digital Currency

The Central Bank of Nigeria (CBN) announced its intention to introduce the eNaira, a digital currency, in 2021. In order to do so, the CBN has formed a partnership with Bitt Inc., a global FinTech company, which will act as the technical partner in this initiative.

This is not the first time that Bitt Inc. has been involved in delivering a digital currency offered by a central bank: in 2019, the Eastern Caribbean Central Bank also collaborated with Bitt Inc. to introduce the CBDC, DCash.

The introduction of the eNaira is aimed at providing monetary support for the Nigerian government and has the potential to contribute to financial stability. During the design phase, the central bank ensured that the eNaira was built upon a stable infrastructure, which is considered to be a fundamental requirement for any payment system. We provide key information on eNaira development in Table 5.4.

Since the official launch of eNaira on October 25, 2021, more than 488,000 consumers have adopted the digital wallet, and around 78,000 merchants from over 160 countries have enrolled. The eNaira has several features that have attracted consumers to it:
- Unlike Bitcoin, eNaira is centralized and regulated.
- eNeira is backed by the Central Bank of Nigeria.
- eNeira is less volatile compared to an unregulated and decentralized cryptocurrency.
- eNeira is exchanged peer to peer.
- eNeira does not yield any interest, making this wallet Shari'ah compliant.

Table 5.4: eNaira at a glance.

Announcement	2021
Status	Launched
CBDC type	Retail
Technology provider	Bitt Inc.
Type of technology used	Hyperledger Fabric

Source: Central Bank of Nigeria (2022)

Purpose of eNaira

The primary purpose for the eNaira is outlined below:
- Facilitate diaspora remittances by providing a secure and cost-effective process for remittances. The CBN is expecting that the eNaira could reduce the amount of remittance flow through informal channels.
- Improve the availability and usability of central bank funds by applying a two-tiered CBDC architecture which provides the CBN with better control of the circulation of eNaira.
- Support a resilient payment system which requires the eNaira to follow the IIERP design principles. IIERP stands for: Inclusive economy, Innovation, Efficient, Resilient, and Proudly Nigerian.

- Encourage financial inclusion by encouraging financial institutions to promote eNaira as a retail payment process.
- Enable direct welfare disbursements to citizens by sending direct payments to eligible citizens under the welfare program. eNaira ensures greater accountability and could allow the Nigerian government to tackle a liquidity crisis in times of financial crisis. For example, the COVID-19 crisis required the government to act to ensure the financial well-being of citizens under the welfare system. eNaira could allow the government to make targeted welfare payments to citizens directly, eliminating the involvement of intermediaries.
- Reduce cost and improve the efficiency of cross-border transactions to ensure Nigeria maintains a vital position in cross-border trade in Africa. The current international payment system is limiting such potential due to its slow and expensive exchange process.

eNaira Infrastructure

There are three parties involved in the development and distribution of eNaira. First, Bitt Inc. provides technical support. The Central Bank of Nigeria serves the role of the regulatory body. Finally, the National Bank of Belize serves as the local basis for the digital currency launch. One of the primary reasons for the CBN to partner with the local bank is to overcome the obstacle of customer adoption of digital currencies.

The eNaira uses the structure of a digital wallet system. Customers are required to download the digital wallet from the dedicated website of the partner bank. One of the main advantages of the digital wallet structure is the use of a blockchain distribution ledger to ensure security for online transactions. Blockchain and distributive ledger technology (DTL) are not similar. While a blockchain itself is a type of distributive ledger, a DTL is unique as it removes the intermediary party from the proofing process, which offers better scaling options in online transactions. Figure 5.3 presents eNaira infrastructure.

The eNaira follows a two-tiered CBDC architecture. The first tier is the Central Bank of Nigeria which serves the responsibility of issuing eNaira. Under such architecture, the CBN retains control of the eNaira payment system, issues digital currency, manages digital wallets, and maintains a central ledger for all transactions. The second tier involves financial institutions and other payment service providers who serve the role of processing retail payments. The enrolment process for eNaira is simple: To sign up for the eNaira digital wallet, customers are required to provide the information identified in Figure 5.4 for the bank verification number (BVN):

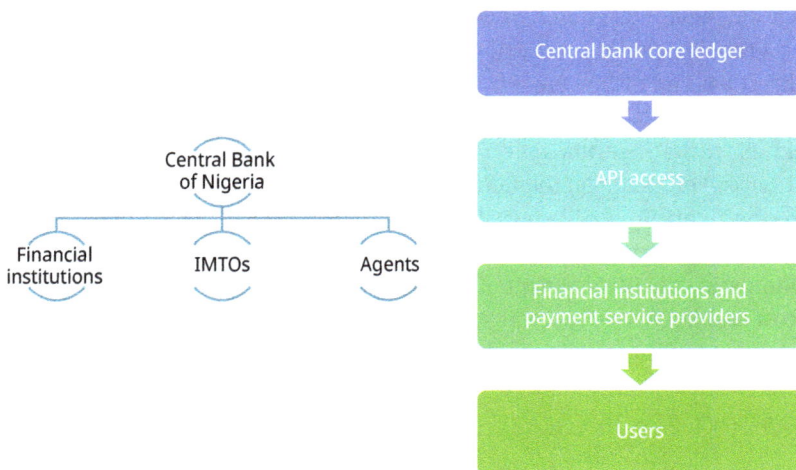

Figure 5.3: eNaira infrastructure.
Source: Central Bank of Nigeria (2022)

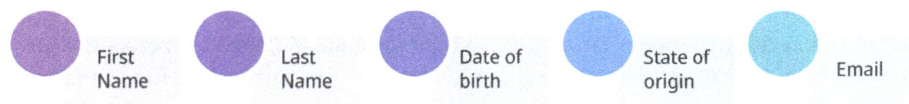

Figure 5.4: The enrolment process for eNaira.
Source: Central Bank of Nigeria (2022)

Types of eNaira

At present, there are three types of eNaira (individual, business and government ministries, departments and agencies (MDAs)) available to meet the demand of many consumers. The differences in the types of eNaira are explained below in Table 5.5:

Risks of eNaira

The CBN has identified several risks associated with the eNaira. These risks include strategic, policy, operational, cybersecurity, and reputational risks. These are outlined below:

– Strategic risks pertain to the potential for disintermediation, which could lead to instability for the eNaira. For the digital currency to be successful, cooperation is required from both households and businesses to convert a portion of their bank

Table 5.5: Types of eNaira.

Feature	For Individuals	For Business	For Government MDAs
Use of eNaira app to open accounts	Yes	No	No
Financial institution verification	Yes	Yes	No
Central bank verification required	No	No	Yes
Number of customer tiers	Four tiers – 0, 1, 2, 3	Tier 4	None
Maximum daily transaction limit	N20,000 – Tier 0 N50,000 – Tier 1 N200,000 – Tier 2 N1,000,000 – Tier 3	N1,000,000	Unlimited
Maximum cumulative daily balance	N120,000 – Tier 0 N300,000 – Tier 1 N500,000 – Tier 2 N5,000,000 – Tier 3	Unlimited	Unlimited

Source: Central Bank of Nigeria (2022)

deposits to eNaira. However, this transfer of existing bank deposits to eNaira digital wallets carries an inherent risk of disintermediation.
–   Policy risks, on the other hand, could limit the future potential of eNaira. The CBN must carefully assess the risk and return of the digital currency, and the risk of disintermediation may require the central bank to implement stringent capital restrictions for banks. The CBN has already restricted the eNaira payment system to micropayments, and the type of policy adopted by the central bank could enhance the attractiveness of the eNaira among Nigerian consumers.
–   Operational risks could affect the daily operations of the eNaira payment system. These risks are related to the design of the eNaira and include legal considerations, stakeholder obligations, responsibility to risk, intellectual property rights, the internal operation of the central bank effectiveness of the IT infrastructure, governance, the decision-making process, and risks related to third-party operations.
–   Cybersecurity risks are always present with digital payment systems, and the eNaira faces numerous cybersecurity risks. The CBN requires a careful assessment of cyber vulnerability to ensure stakeholder trust in this innovative digital currency. These risks include loss by cryptocurrency exchanges from cyberattacks and fraudulent schemes by individuals and criminal syndicates. The CBN provides IT security governance to protect the eNaira from cybersecurity risks, which includes regular IT security assessments to identify vulnerabilities, the implementation of strong internal control measures, and the overall enhancement of security on the platform.

– Reputational risks are also a concern as the eNaira payment system could suffer from reputational issues in case of a failed launch or deployment of the eNaira system. The reputational risk poses an additional challenge for the CBN as it is not quantifiable. Therefore, the CBN needs additional measures to ensure monetary and financial stability through the eNaira.

Digital Ruble: The Bank of Russia's Digital Currency

The Bank of Russia (BoR) is planning to introduce a digital ruble that will possess all the fundamental characteristics of money. Currently, the BoR envisions that the digital ruble will serve as an additional mode of currency and intends to circulate it alongside both cash and non-cash forms of the ruble. The cash ruble is issued by the BoR, whereas non-cash rubles include funds held with the BoR and commercial banks.

The digital ruble, a CBDC, will be issued by the BoR in the form of specialized electronic wallets, each with a unique digital identifier. A notable feature of the digital ruble is the flexibility it affords users during transfers. The digital ruble is often referred to as digital cash due to its resemblance to cash. The stages of digital rubel implementation is available in Figure 5.5.

The BoR is also considering the possibility of allowing users to trade the digital ruble in offline mode; however, this would necessitate additional expenditure on the development of specialized infrastructure. Key stakeholders in the development of the digital ruble include businesses, the public, financial market participants, and the state. The distinctions between the digital ruble and cash are outlined in Table 5.6. Table 5.7 presents the key considerations when designing a digital ruble.

Table 5.6: Differences in features between digital ruble and cash.

	Digital Ruble	Cash
Form	Digital code	Protected paper
Issuer	Central bank	Central bank
Medium of exchange	Online	Not available in online form
Stability	Stable	Stable
Store of value	No interest in accrued	No interest is accrued, and permanent loss is possible

Source: Bank of Russia (2020)

Redistribution of Funds into Central Bank Digital Currency

We demonstrate the redistribution process of funds from cash and bank account into central bank digital currency in Table 5.8 below:

Table 5.7: Essential considerations while designing a digital ruble.

No.	Factors	Remarks
1	User properties	It is important to ensure a digital ruble meets customer demand and protects user rights.
2	Maintaining price and financial stability in the interest of society	The Bank of Russia plans to introduce the digital ruble gradually, allowing the financial industry enough time to adjust to the digital currency.
3	Models and mechanisms	It is important to review the functional capability of the design model chosen for the digital ruble.
4	Ensuring information security	It is important to ensure the information security of the digital ruble.
5	Legal and regulatory changes	It is important to review and develop, if needed, a legal basis before launching the digital ruble.

Source: Bank of Russia (2020)

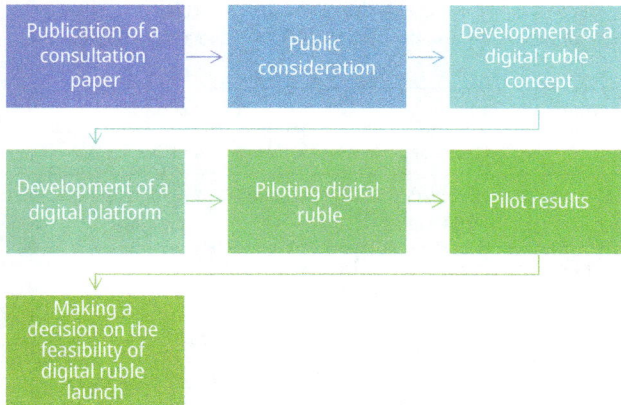

Figure 5.5: Stages of digital ruble implementation.
Source: Bank of Russia (2020)

Bank of Korea's CBDC Initiative

South Korea was the first country to launch a retail fast payment system in 2001 (Bank of Korea, 2022). The nation's financial sector has steadily adopted digital payment systems, due in part to the financial stability enabled by the central bank's scrutiny of the sector, which has improved the efficiency of payment services and enhanced financial inclusion. As a result, the Bank of Korea (BOK) has not deemed it necessary to introduce a CBDC as of yet.

Table 5.8: Redistribution of Funds into Central Bank Digital Currency.

Scenario 1: Cash into CBDC

Such a redistribution of cash to CBDC will affect the balance sheet of the CBDC user and the central bank. The commercial bank's account will remain unchanged, irrespective of their role in transferring the funds.

Household		Commercial Bank		Central Bank	
Asset	Liabilities	Asset	Liabilities	Asset	Liabilities
Deposits	Others	Loans	Deposits	CB operations	Correspondent accounts
CBDC +100 rubles		Correspondent account	CB loans	Others	CBDC +100 rubles
Cash −100 rubles		Others	Capital		Cash −100 rubles
0	0	–	–	0	0

Scenario 2: Commercial Bank Account into CBDC

Such a transfer of funds from a commercial bank account to the CBDC will affect the commercial bank's assets and liability sides. This type of transaction will reduce the bank's balance sheet balance, the user will have a redistribution of funds on their asset side, and the central bank will have a redistribution on the liability side.

Household		Commercial Bank		Central Bank	
Asset	Liabilities	Asset	Liabilities	Asset	Liabilities
Deposits -100 rubles	Others	Loans	Deposits -100 rubles	CB operations	Correspondent accounts −100 rubles
CBDC +100 rubles		Correspondent account −100 rubles	CB loan	Others	CBDC +100 rubles
Cash		Other	Capital		Cash
0	0	−100 rubles	−100 rubles	0	0

However, recent initiatives from the central banks of major developed nations, such as the United States, Europe, China, and Japan, have prompted the BOK to review the implications of a CBDC for the Korean economy. Key considerations for the introduction of a CBDC in South Korea include:

- The decline in the use of cash: In recent years, there has been a global shift in the proportion of cash used in retail transactions in comparison to credit card usage. While European countries are shifting towards cashless transactions, such a trend is not yet prevalent among Korean consumers. The BOK is currently assessing cash usage and credit card transactions. An increase in credit card usage in retail transactions increases transaction fees and fraud risks, which may necessitate the introduction of a digital currency as an alternative universal means of payment. If the BOK considers introducing a CBDC, it should ensure that the currency possesses basic qualities such as reliability, cost-effectiveness, universal acceptance, and safety.

– The market dominance of big tech firms: The market presence of large technology companies in South Korea is growing. Their presence in the electronic commerce and retail payment service sector could influence the central bank's position towards a CBDC, as there is a growing concern that these firms could abuse their dominant position in the platform business. The introduction of a CBDC could prove to be a strategic and regulatory initiative by the central bank to address the potential adverse effects of the market dominance of big tech firms.

– The concentration of personal information: One of the main concerns regarding the introduction of a CBDC is the protection of customers' personal information. A CBDC could allow the central bank to introduce stricter restrictions on personal information protection for financial institutions.

– The proliferation of global cryptocurrencies: The crypto market has not developed as extensively in South Korea as it has in other parts of the world. The development of a CBDC could be linked to the growth of the demand for digital asset-related payments, which are currently managed via bank deposits in South Korea.

Project Aber: Saudi Arabia and United Arab Emirates' Digital Currency

The central banks of Saudi Arabia and the United Arab Emirates jointly initiated Project Aber, a digital currency based on distributed ledger technology (DLT). The project aimed to explore the viability of a dual-issued digital currency that could enable cross-border payments between the two countries. The initiative sought to gain a deeper understanding of DLT and its maturity, with commercial banks actively participating to ensure full involvement from a technical and business perspective. Real money was used in the project, necessitating the examination of non-functional aspects, such as security and the interaction of the system with existing payment systems. The project confirmed the technical feasibility of DLT as a mechanism for both domestic and cross-border settlement and the viability of a single digital currency issued by both central banks. Figure 5.6 illustrates the objectives of Project Aber.

A pilot project was undertaken in which commercial banks pledged real money from their deposits with the central bank to fund their digital currency accounts on the distributed ledger. This provided valuable insights, including feedback from the banks on additional features and improvements that would be required or beneficial in managing a CBDC of this type in the future. A key mandate of the project was to design a solution that was decentralized to the maximum extent possible, as outlined in the motivations for the project.

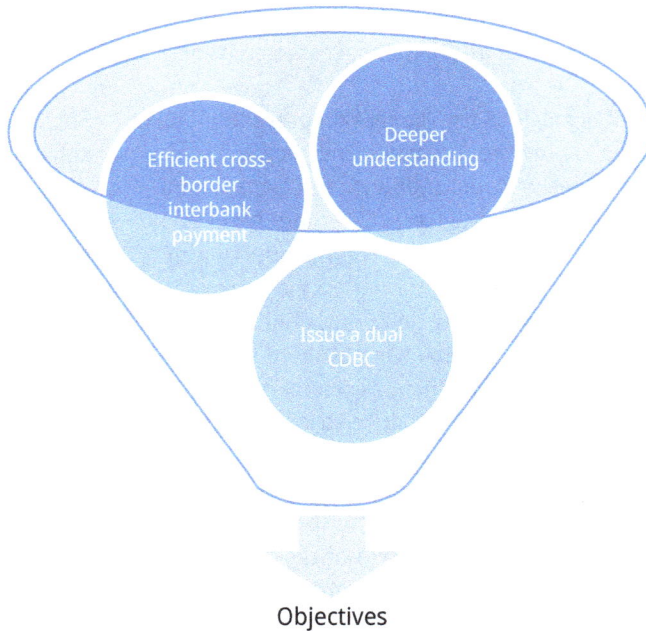

Objectives

Figure 5.6: Key objectives of Project Aber.
Source: Saudi Central Bank and Central Bank of the UAE (2021)

Phases of Project Aber

In Phase 1 (depicted in Figure 5.7), central banks created a shared ledger between them on which various digital currency transactions could take place. Phase 2 addressed domestic payments between commercial banks in each country, while Phase 3 extended this to allow cross-border transactions. The project was carried out in agile sprints with design, development, and operations phases of the three use cases overlapping. The first major milestone was the full implementation of Use Case 1, followed by a three-month operations phase. In parallel, the development of Use Cases 2 and 3 was completed in July 2019.

Key design principles adopted in Project Aber:
- Minimize business impact on as-is systems: It was determined that any modifications to the current systems or procedures might result in unaffordable delays and disruptions. The system needed to interact in some ways with already existing systems, such as real-time gross settlement (RTGS), in the core banking systems. The impact on corporate operations and production systems should be as little as possible.

- Decentralize with safety: Project Aber's vision is for a new payment system that puts more emphasis on decentralization than what is currently offered by the two countries' current payment infrastructure. Whereas current systems are subject to a single point of failure due to centralization, the Aber network should be resilient to such points of failure and allow transactions to be executed without the direct involvement of central banks.
- Scalable design: The system should be able to scale to accommodate the probable transaction volumes involved in at-scale deployment.
- Incentivize use of digital currency: Commercial banks' needs should come first when making design decisions about the currency. Requirements that will maximize the system's utility and usefulness should be given priority. Many requirements, such as using the same currency for domestic and cross-border payments, were formulated based on this.
- Secure and private by design: In a typical banking system, central banks can see all the accounts which commercial banks that hold accounts with them have, but each commercial bank has its own set of accounts. As a design principle, commercial banks should not have visibility into each other's balances. In general, the system should not require a material compromise in privacy.

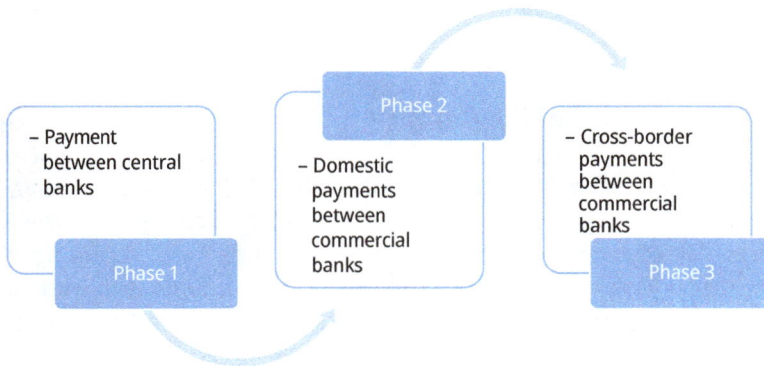

Figure 5.7: Three phases of executing Project Aber.
Source: Saudi Central Bank and Central Bank of UAE (2021)

Digital Euro: The European Union's Digital Currency

The European Union (EU) and European Central Bank (ECB) are currently in development of the digital euro, with proposed strategies officially announced in October 2020 through the release of the ECB's report on a digital euro. The report covers all critical aspects of the digital euro's development, including its concept, scenarios, design and functionality, proposed infrastructure, and operational and institutional framework.

The ECB has three critical aspects in mind when developing scenarios for the digital euro:
- Firstly, it believes a digital euro could improve current economic policies of the EU and reach the objectives of central bank functions.
- Secondly, it would act as a support and boost to the future digitalization of the EU's economy.
- Thirdly, it would have the flexibility to adapt and implement alternative solutions to digital euro.

The ECB has presented two potential approaches through seven scenarios in their report, the first being a centralized approach where transactions are recorded in a centralized ledger operated by the central bank, and the second being a decentralized approach where transactions are settled and recorded by intermediaries under the supervision of the ECB. The design of the digital euro must follow the core principles of the euro monetary policies and the characteristics of online and offline usability and compatibility. Ten general considerations will guide the design of the digital euro, including access model, privacy, limiting or disincentivizing large-scale use as an investment, restrictions, transfer mechanism, payment device, offline usability, remuneration, legal tender, and parallel infrastructure. We provide a detailed analysis on the digital euro in Chapter 6.

Digital Yuan: China's Digital Currency

The primary purpose of China's digital currency – officially called the digital currency electronic payment (DCEP), commonly referred to as the digital yuan – is to improve and digitalize everyday payments and serve as a replacement for cash. According to Yeung (2020), the digital yuan will enable users to conduct transactions even without an internet connection, enabling it to closely replicate cash transactions. There is significant interest in the technologies that will enable the usage of the digital yuan as it is one of the first and most developed CBDCs.

The digital yuan's framework is different from other privately developed cryptocurrencies and utilizes a two-tier system, where commercial banks are responsible for distributing the currency to consumers. The digital yuan framework is divided into three parts: the central bank, commercial banks, and end users. The central bank is responsible for issuing the currency, handling verifications and registrations, and managing liquidity. Commercial banks are delegated operational tasks, such as customer service, and end users are only involved in deposit and withdrawal. The overall aim of the framework is to provide a well-functioning digital currency at all levels. We provide a detailed analysis on the digital yuan in Chapter 7.

E-dinar: The Central Bank of Tunisia's Digital Currency

Since 2016, the Central Bank of Tunisia (BCT) has been experimenting with the use of the electronic dinar, also known as the e-dinar. The e-dinar project aims to advance financial inclusion and the nation's digital transformation. The Tunisian e-dinar can be used to make payments to the government as well as conduct digital transactions between people and businesses using the e-dinar.

Blockchain technology, on which the e-dinar is based, enables the safe and open tracking of transactions. The BCT has also put in place a mechanism that allows authorized agents to convert physical dinar into e-dinar and vice versa. The BCT intends to increase the use of the e-dinar in the future after testing it with a small number of users during a pilot phase. In order to boost the effectiveness and security of the nation's financial system even further, the BCT intends to connect the e-dinar with other digital services, such as digital ID and digital signature. The e-dinar has not yet been made available to the general public and the status of the project is unknown.

Project Icebreaker

Project Icebreaker, a collaboration between the Bank for International Settlements (BIS) and the central banks of Israel, Norway, and Sweden, contributes significantly to the ongoing discussions on the use of CBDCs in cross-border payments, including cross-currency payments, by identifying crucial technical and policy decisions that central banks need to consider in their exploration of CBDCs. The BIS Innovation Hub's cross-border CBDC projects, such as Jura, Dunbar, and mBridge, have explored various approaches to enhancing cross-border payments by issuing several wholesale CBDCs on multilateral platforms.

However, Project Icebreaker takes a different approach, using a hub-and-spoke solution to connect various retail CBDC (rCBDC) DLT-based systems. Although it shares some similarities with Project Nexus (see next section), which interconnects domestic instant payment systems, Project Icebreaker differs in terms of its settlement method, choice of FX provider, use of bridge currencies, and the technologies used in each domestic system.

There are different ways of connecting disparate systems, including single access, bilateral linking, and hub-and-spoke solutions. Project Icebreaker used a hub-and-spoke solution to interlink domestic rCBDC systems via a technical platform that facilitates communication between the systems. This solution requires each rCBDC system to integrate with the Icebreaker hub only, instead of integrating with each rCBDC system. The hub-and-spoke solution can scale up to accommodate many participating systems without increasing complexity. Domestic rCBDC systems can connect to the hub in two ways, allowing system participants, like wallet and FX providers, to communicate with the hub directly, or using the domestic rCBDC system as a gateway to serve as a single communication channel between the domestic rCBDC system and the hub.

Project Nexus

Over 60 countries have instant payment systems allowing for fast transfers between people, but cross-border payments are still slow and costly. Project Nexus aims to connect these national payment systems to create a cross-border platform and improve the speed, cost, and transparency of cross-border payments. The project is moving to the testing phase, with the Monetary Authority of Singapore, Bank of Italy, Central Bank of Malaysia, Banking Computer Services, and PayNet working together to test connecting the payment systems of Singapore, Malaysia, and the euro area. Nexus standardizes connections between payment systems, providing a more scalable way to grow instant cross-border payment networks. The testing phase will explore the potential for Nexus to ease and speed up the process of linking fast payment systems.

Similarities between CBDCs around the world

The central bank of a nation issues and backs CBDCs, which are digital representations of that nation's currency. There are some global parallels in the features and traits of CBDCs, even though the precise design and functionality may differ between nations. Several of these parallels include:
- All of them are digital representations of a nation's national currency that the central bank issues and backs.
- They are all designed to offer a secure and effective method of processing digital payments.
- To keep track of transactions, they all make use of distributed ledger technologies, such as blockchain.
- All of them strive to broaden financial inclusion and decrease the use of cash.
- Compared to other digital payment options, they all provide a higher level of security, traceability, and monitoring.
- They could all encounter regulatory obstacles including money laundering, terrorism financing, and consumer protection.

Chapter Summary

- Central bank digital currencies (CBDCs) are being created and used all over the world. CBDCs have the potential to boost financial inclusion and increase payment system efficiency and security.

- As a result of Project Sand Dollar in December 2019, the Central Bank of the Bahamas introduced the Sand Dollar, a digital version of the Bahamian dollar.
- The digital ruble is often referred to as digital cash due to its resemblance to cash. It will be issued in the form of specialized electronic wallets, each with a unique digital identifier.
- South Korea was the first country to launch a retail fast payment system in 2001.
- The introduction of the eNaira is aimed at providing monetary support for the Nigerian government and has the potential to contribute to financial stability.
- Project Aber aimed to explore the viability of a dual-issued digital currency that could enable cross-border payments.
- The European Union and European Central Bank are currently in development of the digital euro.
- China's digital currency, the digital currency electronic payment (DCEP), is one of the first and most developed CBDCs.
- The Tunisia's e-dinar project aims to advance financial inclusion and the nation's digital transformation.

Discussion Questions

- How might CBDCs specifically affect the function of commercial banks and the use of actual cash?
- How might CBDCs affect financial stability and monetary policy? What are the possible hazards involved with central banks using CBDCs to carry out monetary policy and how might they do so?
- How might the emergence of CBDCs affect cross-border transactions and global trade? What potential difficulties can arise from using CBDCs to promote international trade?
- How might the use of CBDCs affect data security and privacy? What possible problems could arise from central banks and other authorities collecting and using data, and how might these risks be reduced?
- How can the emergence of CBDCs affect the current global monetary competitiveness and the US dollar's status as a reserve currency?
- How might CBDCs be employed in global monetary politics and economic statecraft?

Learn from the Web

The following resources provide information on CBDC development around the world:

- Bank for International Settlements (BIS): https://www.bis.org/about/bisih/topics/cbdc.htm
- International Monetary Fund (IMF): https://www.imf.org/en/Publications/fandd/issues/2022/09/Picture-this-The-ascent-of-CBDCs
- The People's Bank of China: http://www.pbc.gov.cn/en/3688110/3688172/4157443/4293696/2021071614584691871.pdf
- European Central Bank: https://www.ecb.europa.eu/paym/digital_euro/html/index.en.html
- Bank of Japan:
- https://www.boj.or.jp/en/paym/digital/index.htm
- The Digital Currency Initiative (DCI) at the MIT Media Lab: https://www.media.mit.edu/projects/central-banks-and-digital-currency/overview/
- The Cambridge Centre for Alternative Finance (CCAF): https://www.jbs.cam.ac.uk/faculty-research/centres/alternative-finance/

References

Arnold, M. (2 October, 2020). ECB confident it can overcome challenges to create a digital euro. *Financial Times*. Available at: https://www.ft.com/content/b6f0c233-0b35-45d1-896f-1c6599558d9b

Bae, J. (2022). The Bank of Korea's CBDC research: current status and key considerations. In BIS Papers, 107. Available at: https://www.bis.org/publ/bppdf/bispap123_m.pdf

Bank of Russia (2020). A Digital Ruble. [Online] Available at: https://cbr.ru/eng/analytics/d_ok/dig_ruble/

CBDC Tracker (2023). Today's Central Bank Digital Currencies Status. Available at: https://cbdctracker.org/

Central Bank of Bahamas (2018). Analysis of the Bahamas Financial Literacy Survey 2018. Available at: https://www.centralbankbahamas.com/news/general-news/analysis-of-the-bahamas-financial-literacy-survey-2018

Central Bank of Bahamas (2019). Project Sand Dollar: A Bahamas Payments System Modernisation Initiative. Available at: https://www.centralbankbahamas.com/viewPDF/documents/2019-12-25-02-18-11-Project-Sanddollar.pdf

Central Bank of Jamaica (2023). Jamaica's Central Bank Digital Currency (CBDC) – JAM-DEX. Available at: https://boj.org.jm/core-functions/currency/cbdc/

Central Bank of Nigeria (2022). eNaira. [Online] Available at: https://www.cbn.gov.ng/currency/enaira.asp

East Caribbean Central Bank (2021). The ECCB's Digital Currency (DCash) is a Critical Step in the Buildout of a Digital Economy in the ECCU. Available at: https://www.eccb-centralbank.org/blog/view/the-eccbas-digital-currency-dcash-is-a-critical-step-in-the-buildout-of-a-digital-economy-in-the-eccu

Fanusie, Y.J. and Jin, E. (2021). China's Digital Currency: Adding Financial Data to Digital Authoritarianism. Avaiable at: https://www.cnas.org/publications/reports/chinas-digital-currency

Saudi Central Bank and Central Bank of the UAE (2021). Project Aber. [Online] Available at: https://www.sama.gov.sa/en-US/News/Documents/Project_Aber_report-EN.pdf

Yueng, K. (2020). What is China's sovereign digital currency? [Online] Available at: https://www.scmp.com/economy/china-economy/article/3083952/what-chinas-cryptocurrency-sovereign-digital-currency-and-why

Further Reading

Coulter, K. A. (2023). A Review of the Proposed Bank of England's "Retail" Central Bank Digital Currency (CBDC) as a Cryptocurrency Competitor. *Fintech, Pandemic, and the Financial System: Challenges and Opportunities*, 22, 201–221.

Kuehnlenz, S., Orsi, B., & Kaltenbrunner, A. (2023). Central bank digital currencies and the international payment system: The demise of the US dollar?. *Research in International Business and Finance*, 64, 101834.

Lee, C. C., Wang, C. W., Hsieh, H. Y., & Chen, W. L. (2023). The impact of central bank digital currency variation on firm's implied volatility. *Research in International Business and Finance*, 101878.

Merrell, I. (2022). Blockchain for decentralised rural development and governance. *Blockchain: Research and Applications*, 3(3), 100086.

Syarifuddin, F. (2023). Optimal Central Bank Digital Currency (CBDC) Design for Emerging Economies. Available at *SSRN 4321306*.

Tan, E., Mahula, S., & Crompvoets, J. (2022). Blockchain governance in the public sector: A conceptual framework for public management. *Government Information Quarterly*, 39(1), 101625.

6 The Digital Euro

Key Facts on the Digital Euro
- Around 80% of European citizens were aware of the idea of a digital euro, and 70% supported it, according to a 2019 survey by the European Central Bank (ECB).
- Improving financial inclusion and accessibility, especially for those who are currently unbanked or underbanked, is one of the primary drivers for a digital euro.
- A digital euro may boost the effectiveness of international transactions and make the payment system more resilient to online assaults.
- According to the ECB, a digital euro would supplement currency rather than substitute it.
- The ECB is now investigating the advantages, dangers, and design of a digital euro and consulting the general public in the process.

Introduction

According to Sandbu (2020), the advent of central bank digital currencies (CBDCs) is not a question of if, but rather when the first CBDC will officially be released to the public. A CBDC could bring many benefits and help to attract fresh investments to a particular country. One of the first CBDCs currently in development is the digital euro, developed by the European Union (EU) and the European Central Bank (ECB).

The proposed strategies for the digital euro were officially announced in October 2020 with the release of the ECB's report on a digital euro. Subsequently, there have been several smaller updates published by the ECB until late 2022. To gain a comprehensive understanding of the position and the process of the digital euro, this chapter serves as a foundational reference. The contents of the ECB report and its updates present all critical aspects of digital euro development, including its concept, possible scenarios, design and functionality, proposed infrastructure, operational and institutional framework, and initial outcomes of the investigation stage. All of these aspects, including observations from other sources, will be studied in this chapters.

The ECB's Scenarios for the Digital Euro

When developing possible scenarios for a digital euro, the ECB (2020) identified three critical considerations.
- Firstly, the digital euro could potentially achieve the objectives of central bank functions and enhance current economic policies within the EU.
- Secondly, the ECB believes that the issuance of a digital euro could serve as a support and boost to the future digitalization of the EU's economy. In this vein, the implementation of a CBDC would act as a response to the decline in the use of

https://doi.org/10.1515/9783110982398-006

cash and could also mitigate the risk of the euro being overtaken by foreign or private CBDCs.
– Thirdly, the ECB contends that a digital euro could serve as a new monetary policy transmission channel, thereby helping to mitigate risks associated with digital payments and cybersecurity.

Overall, a digital euro would support lower currency costs and reduce its ecological footprint. Arnold (2020) has studied the ECB's report on a digital euro and highlighted two potential approaches:
– The first approach is based on centralized scenarios, in which all digital euro transactions would be recorded in a centralized ledger operated by the central bank.
– The second approach – decentralized scenarios – would see transactions settled and recorded by intermediaries, which would be under the supervision of the ECB.

The first group of possible scenarios relates to core central bank functions, while the second group relates to other objectives of the EU. For each of the proposed scenarios, the ECB has outlined the specific area that would be improved or solved by the introduction of a digital euro. Furthermore, the ECB has provided requirements for each proposed scenario, which must be met in order for the proposed scenario to be deemed beneficial in comparison to current fiat currencies. The timeline of the digital euro is provided in Table 6.1 below:

Table 6.1: The timeline of the digital euro.

2018	The European Central Bank (ECB) declared it would start looking into the prospect of releasing a digital euro.
2019	The public consultation on the digital euro was opened by the ECB.
2020	Phase 1 of the ECB's digital euro project, which concentrated on technical and functional criteria, was launched.
2021	Phase 2 of the ECB's digital euro project, which examines the possible advantages and hazards of a digital euro, was launched.
2022	Depending on how Phase 2 turns out, the ECB intends to run a substantial trial of the digital euro.
2023	Depending on the results of Phase 2 and the large-scale trial, the ECB will decide whether to move forward with issuing a digital euro.

Approaches from the ECB's Standpoint

In order to ensure these benefits are realized, the ECB has also identified specific requirements that must be met during the development process. These requirements, which are essential for the establishment of a secure and stable digital currency, must be satisfied in order for the digital euro to be a viable replacement for fiat currency in the future. In Table 6.2, the most critical aspects of each scenario are presented for further analysis.

Table 6.2: Critical aspects of various scenarios on a digital euro.

Scenario	Need	Requirement
Benefits of CBDC in terms of digitalization and independence of the EU economy.	CBDC supports attracting new digital companies and enabling the further growth of digitalization and the FinTech industry.	Digital euro must be constantly updated with the latest technologies that will make it attractive for the industry.
Declining use of cash as a means of payment.	Suppose further cash decline as a means of payment that increases the independence of private forms of money. CBDC should resolve that and give users in the EU another cash-like means of digital payments.	Digital euro should replicate the main features of cash. An important aspect would be the ability of offline payments that would mimic the use of physical cash.
Access or acceptance of non-euro-denominated digital money.	Make digital euro available through third-party infrastructures and offer acceptance of other non-euro-denominated currencies.	Digital euro features should be at the tech frontier. Its functionalities need to be more attractive than other payment solutions of foreign currencies.
Digital euro issuance is beneficial from a monetary policy perspective.	CBDC issuance enable the central banks to set the remuneration rate on the digital euro to directly influence the consumption and investment choices of the non-financial sector.	Digital euro could be used to improve the transmission of monetary policy. It needs to be remunerated at the interest rate, allowing the central bank to change it in the future.
Mitigation of probability of extreme events which could significantly impact CBDC stability.	Natural disasters, medical emergencies (including pandemics), and cybersecurity risks are a threat to the current payments system. A digital euro, combined with cash, could create a contingency mechanism that could stay in use even when private options might be unavailable.	To lessen the impact of these threats, the digital euro should be widely used and accepted. It has to be transacted through its channels. That would allow for its independence from other payment systems and would allow the CBDC to overcome extreme events.

Source: Adapted from the ECB report on a digital euro (2020).

Approaches that Affect Other EU Objectives

The ECB has separated the two scenarios (see Table 6.3) as they do not directly relate to the central bank's core functions. The Treaty on the Functioning of the European Union (TFEU) states that to establish a functioning digital euro, it must contribute towards the broader objectives of the EU.

Table 6.3: Digital euro approaches that affect other EU objectives.

Scenario	Need	Requirement
Digital euro's international role.	The high importance of keeping the euro as a stable international currency. Needs to improve and reinforce the EU's monetary authority.	Accessibility of digital euro outside the euro area.
Eurosystem's decision to support the overall improvement costs and monetary ecological footprint.	Design, developments and maintenance should be energy and resource efficient. It needs to be well designed to reduce the overall costs.	Cost reduction should be achieved, compared to the current payments system. Design should be based on solutions that minimize the ecological footprint.

Source: Adapted from the ECB report on a digital euro (2020)

As evidenced in Table 6.3, the two scenarios presented are entirely disparate. The ECB has expressed an ambition to develop the digital euro into a global digital currency as well. However, it is unlikely that such an aspiration would be achievable in the early stages of development, as it may prove to be too complex. Nevertheless, if the digital euro proves to be a successful digital currency, there may be potential for global expansion in the future.

An important consideration in relation to global expansion is the ecological footprint of digital currencies. The maintenance of banknotes and coins results in a substantial ecological footprint. Therefore, it is crucial that the new digital currency is designed in a way that reduces this impact. A central focus should be placed on energy efficiency, as digital currencies are primarily reliant on electricity to power servers and cloud services. As demonstrated by the example of Bitcoin, electricity consumption is one of the main cost drivers. Thus, reducing the electricity consumption of the digital euro should be a key priority in its development.

Design Possibilities of the Digital Euro

When designing a new type of digital currency that has not been developed yet, certain key considerations must be taken into account. The ECB has identified two primary considerations in its report. The first is the adherence to core principles of euro monetary policies and their associated requirements. The second consideration that the ECB has outlined is the compatibility of both online and offline characteristics of the digital currency, and the need for these characteristics to satisfy requirements and core economic principles. The ECB has formulated 10 general considerations that will guide the design of the digital euro. The ECB has carefully studied several key design considerations for the development of a digital euro. These considerations will now be briefly presented.

One consideration is the access model for consumers. According to the ECB, consumers could have direct access to their digital euros, facilitated through the provision of consumer identification and customer support solutions by the central bank. Alternatively, an indirect access option could be adopted, in which access to the digital euro is facilitated through intermediaries, such as commercial banks, without the need for additional services to be developed by the central bank.

In order to prevent excessive shifts of fiat money into the digital euro, the ECB and Eurosystem are also considering limiting the use of the digital euro for investment purposes. This may involve setting limits on the maximum amount of digital euro that can be held, or limiting access to the digital euro for certain individuals or enterprises, such as foreign residents or visitors staying in the EU, who would only be able to hold digital euros during their stay in the Eurosystem. These limitations are believed to be a genuine possibility in the initial stages of the digital euro's implementation, as they would make implementation less cumbersome and prevent the digital euro from being used globally, where other risks and rules would apply.

The transfer mechanism for the digital euro presents two options: an account-based system or a "bearer instrument." According to the ECB, in an account-based system, third parties would record users' holdings and determine the validity of transactions, updating the respective balances on behalf of the payer and payee. This is the approach currently employed by major electronic payment solutions and would allow the central bank issuing the CBDC to control transaction flows. However, this method would be inapplicable in situations where users or the central third party are not online.

In contrast, the bearer instrument approach would involve the payer and payee being responsible for verifying the transfer of value between them, similar to how cash payments function. This approach would fall outside the direct control of the Eurosystem or its supervised intermediaries, with limits on holdings and on the value of international transactions, as well as restrictions on the target group of users only able to be enforced at the payment device level.

Payment devices refer to the ways in which the central bank will offer digital euros to consumers, with options including web-based services or physical devices such as smart cards. These options can also be combined, with web-based services easily accessible through various smart devices as long as there is an internet connection. Physical devices, on the other hand, would require a specific device compatible for offline use without an internet connection. Combining the two options would provide the best solution as it would allow for offline transactions to be possible.

One of the most crucial aspects of the digital euro is its offline usability, as it allows consumers to utilize the currency in a manner similar to cash, while also enabling anonymous transactions. To ensure the integrity of these offline transactions, they can be verified through the use of hardware that is trusted by the provider of the digital euro. This offline functionality also serves as a backup payment solution in extreme circumstances, and can be facilitated through the use of smart cards, mobile devices, or payment terminals. Furthermore, the transactions are settled immediately, as the hardware is pre-funded, similar to pre-funded credit cards.

 The remuneration of a digital euro may be implemented for both monetary policy and structural reasons in order to maintain the financial stability of the currency and mitigate demand and price. However, the ECB notes that remuneration may also be viewed as an attractive feature for users, though it may be at odds with the central bank's monetary policy objectives.

In terms of infrastructure, the digital euro will be based on parallel systems of other payment solutions, which will enhance its position in extreme situations that may affect and disable other currently used means of payments. However, private providers may find it cost-prohibitive to establish such parallel infrastructure, particularly due to the high initial costs involved. Additionally, the ECB must take into account the magnitude and probability of extreme events when considering the viability of a parallel system and infrastructure, as well as the efficiency and environmental impact.

Current State and Future Position of the Digital Euro

According to Arnold (2020), the ECB is currently in the consultation phase regarding the introduction of a digital euro and has yet to make a final decision. This decision is expected to be made following the analysis of results from a public consultation, which occured in the middle of 2021. However, the ECB has stated that experimental projects and development will proceed regardless of the outcome of the final decision. In April 2021, the ECB published the first responses to the concluded public consultation in order to gain a better understanding of public opinion on the development of CBDCs and potential scenarios for a digital euro.

According to Arnold, a significant percentage of respondents prioritized the privacy of their payments, highlighting the importance of cash and its anonymity. ECB should introduce a CBDC that possesses cash-like features, specifically the ability to conduct offline transactions without internet connectivity. In October 2021, the ECB announced that development is continuing with the investigative phase.

According to Panetta (2021), if the ECB receives approval to continue development of the digital euro, it could potentially be launched within the next five years. The ECB is currently facing in relation to the digital euro. One of the key issues is the ability of the digital euro to replicate the characteristics of cash, particularly in terms of anonymity. Many respondents have expressed concern that the digital euro could completely replace cash and lead to retailers profiting from customers' transaction data, thereby allowing governments to monitor consumers' activities. As such, the ability to conduct offline payments is considered of paramount importance. Panetta notes that while complete anonymity may not be possible, the ECB is exploring ways to use technology to protect user privacy without compromising standards against illicit activities.

The report also raises the question of whether the digital euro should be offered internationally and positioned as a global digital currency or whether it should be confined to the Eurosystem. Panetta argues that it is essential to establish a well-functioning digital currency within the Eurosystem before considering expansion to foreign countries.

Digital Euro as Strengthening Tool for Fiat Euro

According to Mancini-Griffoli et al. (2018), ensuring price stability in CBDCs is an especially challenging task, particularly in rapidly changing economic circumstances such as global financial crises and pandemics. It has been posited that the presence of cash can constrain interest rate policy, and that cash may only be replaced in the longer term if the implementation of CBDCs is successful.

Stability of CBDCs Compared to Fiat Currency

Adrian and Mancini-Griffoli (2019) have conducted a comparative analysis of the stability of various means of payment in relation to CBDCs. They posit that CBDCs should be closely compared to cash or central bank money, as these are considered optimal as stores of value in normal circumstances. However, it is acknowledged that digital money, including CBDCs, is subject to operational and cyber risks, which are also present in other means of payment. In addition to these common risks, Adrian and Mancini-Griffoli identify four further risks specific to digital money or CBDCs: liquidity risk, market risk, foreign exchange rate risk, and default risk.

To mitigate these risks and improve the stability of CBDCs, Adrian and Mancini-Griffoli propose four solutions. The first solution suggests that central banks should invest more in short-term government papers, with the safest and most liquid assets being central bank reserves. The second solution proposes that the creation of e-money should always be lower or equal to the value of client funds received to prevent overissuance and ensure the ability to meet redemption requests. The third solution recommends that assets held by CBDC issuers should not be encumbered in order to protect consumers in the event of bankruptcy. Finally, it is argued that sufficient capital is required to offset sudden market movements and potential losses that may affect stability.

Can a Digital Euro Help Strengthen the Fiat Euro?

In 2022, the euro area experienced a significant inflation rate that exceeded the typical 2% per annum. This was due to the prevailing economic, geopolitical, and energy crises, which have all contributed to the weakening of the euro, particularly against the US dollar. Consequently, it can be debated whether the introduction of a digital euro could help to fortify the position of the fiat euro.

As the topic of the weakening euro is still a recent one at the time of writing this book, we are unable to confirm or deny whether the digital euro will assist in strengthening its fiat counterpart. This may be one of the key areas of investigation, as discussed in the previous sections. In our opinion, the true impact of the digital euro on its fiat counterpart will only be apparent after its implementation and functionality have been established. However, the implementation of CBDCs on such a large scale has yet to be implemented in any country, making it difficult to predict the effect on the fiat currency.

Chapter Summary

- The advent of central bank digital currencies (CBDCs) is not a question of if, but rather when the first CBDC will officially be released to the public.
- The digital euro is currently being developed by the EU and the ECB.
- A digital euro could potentially achieve the objectives of central bank functions and enhance current economic policies within the EU.
- The transfer mechanism for the digital euro presents two options: an account-based system or a bearer instrument.
- A digital euro could potentially be launched within the next five years.

Discussion Questions
- How does the development and implementation of a digital euro compare to other countries' efforts to create a CBDC?
- What are some of the potential benefits and drawbacks of a digital euro for the European economy and financial system?

- How might a digital euro impact the relationship between the ECD and commercial banks, and what implications might this have for monetary policy?
- What are some of the technical and logistical challenges that will need to be overcome in order to successfully launch a digital euro?
- How might the introduction of a digital euro affect consumer behavior and the use of cash, and what impact might this have on financial inclusion and inequality?
- How can the digital euro be designed to ensure security, privacy, and anti-money laundering measures?
- What are the legal and regulatory challenges that need to be addressed to implement a digital euro?
- What are the implications of a digital euro on cross-border payments and how can it be leveraged to enhance the integration of the EU market?
- How can the digital euro be designed to ensure interoperability with other digital assets and payment systems?
- How can the digital euro be designed to ensure that it is accessible to all citizens, including those who are unbanked or underbanked?

Learn from the Web

The following websites provide valuable insight on the digital euro:

- The European Central Bank's website: https://www.ecb.europa.eu
- The Bank for International Settlements (BIS): https://www.bis.org
- The Centre for International Governance Innovation (CIGI): https://www.cigionline.org
- The International Monetary Fund (IMF): https://www.imf.org/
- The World Economic Forum (WEF): https://www.weforum.org/

References

Adrian, T. & Mancini-Griffoli, T., (2019). The Rise of Digital Money. *IMF FinTech Note No. 19/01*, July, pp.2–12.

Arnold, M., (2 October, 2020). ECB confident it can overcome challenges to create a Digital Euro. *Financial Times*. Available at: https://www.ft.com/content/b6f0c233-0b35-45d1-896f-1c6599558d9b

European Central Bank (2020). Report on a digital euro. Available at: https://www.ecb.europa.eu/pub/pdf/other/Report_on_a_digital_euro~4d7268b458.en.pdf

Mancini-Griffoli, T., Peria, M. S. M., Agur, I., Ari, A., Kiff, J., Popescu, A., & Rochon, C. (2018). Casting light on central bank digital currency. *IMF staff discussion note*, 8(18), 1–39.

Panetta, F., 2021 A digital euro to meet the expectations of Europeans. European Central Bank. Available at: https://www.ecb.europa.eu/press/key/date/2021/html/ecb.sp210414_1~e76b855b5c.en.html

Sandbu, M., 2020. A digital euro is on its way. *Financial Times*. [Online] Available at: https://www.ft.com/content/2b5ad7d5-edf8-4bb5-af77-15eef64dbe53

Further Reading

Brunnermeier, M. K., & Landau, J. P. (2022). The Digital Euro: policy implications and perspectives. European Parliament.

Deutsche Bank (2021), The digital euro: Political ambitions and economic realities. [Online] Available at: https://www.dbresearch.com/PROD/RPS_EN-PROD/PROD0000000000519236/The_digital_euro%3A_

Political_ambitions_and_economic.pdf?undefined&realload=1sTub8r8vDU2/10T6BRTQ8jAHoxBDeJGL~
aOABHexvid6Nqy1Y3L/Alz2EqG76I5

Sandner, P., & Gross, J. (2023). The Digital Euro From a Geopolitical Perspective: Will Europe Lag Behind?
In *Fintech, Pandemic, and the Financial System: Challenges and Opportunities*, 22, 223–240.

Troitiño, D. R. (2022). The European Union Facing the 21st Century: The Digital Revolution. *TalTech Journal
of European Studies*, *12*(1), 60–78.

7 The Digital Yuan

> **Key Facts on the Digital Yuan**
> - The digital yuan is the first central bank digital currency (CBDC) in the history of the world to be widely used.
> - The central bank of China, the People's Bank of China (PBOC), is in charge of creating and administering the digital yuan.
> - The digital yuan is intended to complement physical money rather than replace it.
> - In various Chinese cities, including Shenzhen, Chengdu, Suzhou, and Xiong'an New Area, the digital yuan has been put to the test.
> - A lottery event was held in Shenzhen in October 2020, and winners received 1.5 million US dollars' worth of digital yuan, which they could use at more than 3,000 local businesses.

Introduction

This chapter delves into an examination and analysis of the issuance of the digital yuan. According to Tran and Matthews (2020), China's digital currency is officially referred to as the digital currency electronic payment (DCEP). For consistency in the discussion, we will refer to the DCEP as the digital yuan in this chapter. At first glance, it may appear that the digital euro and digital yuan have similar goals and approaches. However, as with other technologies, the development and objectives of CBDCs vary substantially from country to country. It is worth noting that China was one of the pioneers in the development of CBDCs. China began exploring the development of CBDCs in 2014. The principal motivation behind this was to keep pace with the rapid digitization of financial transactions. China and the digital yuan have set the foundation for other central banks and their CBDC development.

To gain a deeper understanding of the digital yuan, it is essential to comprehend its purpose and objective. According to Yeung (2020), the primary purpose of the digital yuan is to simulate everyday banking activities, including payments, deposits, and withdrawals from a digital wallet. The primary goal of the digital yuan is focused on the improvement and digitalization of everyday payments and the replacement of cash. A digital wallet would ultimately serve as a replacement for cash as a bearer instrument. On the surface, the digital yuan's purpose may resemble that of digital currencies developed by China's tech giants, Alibaba's Alipay and Tencent's WeChat Pay. However, Yeung argues that the digital yuan will also enable users to use it without an internet connection, allowing for offline transactions and closely replicating the functionality of cash. This approach will be a significant benefit over other digital currencies.

https://doi.org/10.1515/9783110982398-007

The Underlying Technology of the Digital Yuan

An essential aspect of the digital yuan is its underlying technology. According to Gantori et al. (2020), the digital yuan will be based on China's blockchain service network (BSN). Gantori et al. (2020) state that the network was launched and will be led by the State Information Center, a government agency under the National Development and Reform Commission, as well as state-owned telecommunication giants including China Telecom and China Unicom, and payments firm China Union Pay. In 2020, the BSN Development Association published an introductory white paper in which the concept of the blockchain-based service network was defined. According to the BSN Development Association (2020), the main objective of the BSN is to provide a global infrastructure based on blockchain.

Its further aim is to provide a public blockchain framework that would lower the development and operational costs. Such a general framework would simplify operations for small local blockchain frameworks that currently encounter high fixed development and operational costs compared to their small size. Gantori et al. suggests that the BSN should act as the primary infrastructure body that will help to lower the costs of blockchain service development, operations, maintenance, and regulation.

The Framework of Blockchain Service Network

To better understand the operational aspect of the BSN, Figure 7.1 summarizes the main components, as outlined by Gantori et al.. Gantori et al. have pointed out two main components. The first is the deployment of public city nodes (PCNs), represented by data centers and cloud computing centers based in cities, which are tasked with processing digital currency transactions. The second component is the configuration and modification of several enterprise blockchain protocols, such as Hyperledger Fabric, or other local protocols to fit a uniform standard. In Figure 7.1, the other three parts of the BSN are also presented, and it is important to note that all of them must work together to make the BSN operational.

The framework of China's BSN is critical to the successful introduction of the digital yuan. The BSN comprises several key components, with Figure 7.1 summarizing the main parts. However, to gain a comprehensive understanding of the BSN's framework, all parts must be considered.

One of the key components of the BSN infrastructure is the deployment of PCNs. The BSN Development Association states that the primary function of PCNs is to provide the BSN with control of access to the digital currency system, storage of data, processing of transactions, and acting as computing support for blockchain applications.

Another important aspect of the BSN is the use of consensus order cluster services as a tool for optimizing running costs. These services can operate using either collective clustering or distributed clustering, which allows for a load-balancing mechanism that

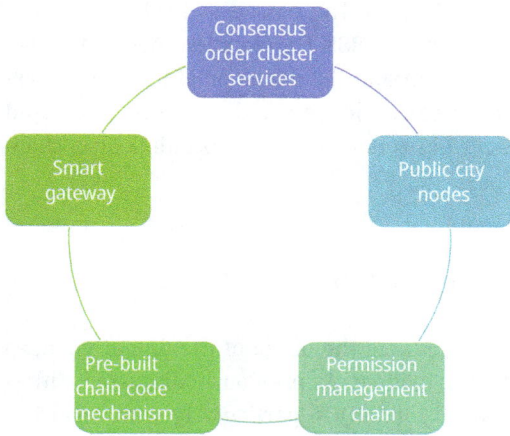

Figure 7.1: Parts of China's blockchain service network (BSN).
Source: Gantori et al. (2020)

calculates different resource configurations for different blockchain-based applications with varying demands, thereby enabling cost optimization.

In addition to these components, the BSN also utilizes a smart gateway to satisfy the diverse needs of different businesses in a blockchain application. This is necessary as relying solely on application chain code may not be sufficient. The smart gateway links a private system to a blockchain system, enabling businesses to have a system based on blockchain. The BSN also employs a pre-built chain code mechanism, which provides configuration and modification of enterprise blockchain protocols.

Additionally, the BSN utilizes a permission management chain, which is a basic, system-level chain used to manage the relationship between the role and permissions configuration of each application. This chain is deployed within each PCN and provides each application with a permission management mechanism that is uniformly stored on the chain, is fully controllable by the developer, and uses application-role-based control (ARBAC). The ARBAC model allows users to have different levels of access, which is integrated into the BSN application, allowing permissions to be automatically designated to the user's account upon accessing the BSN via the PCN.

The BSN Development Association identifies five key areas in which the BSN system offers advantages; however, two of these areas stand out as particularly noteworthy. The first notable advantage is the cost savings that can be achieved through the use of the BSN. The greatest savings can be realized in terms of the initial investment required for issuance. Additionally, following the deployment and development of the BSN, significant cost savings can also be realized in terms of the ongoing operation and maintenance of the system.

The BSN Development Association aims to achieve these savings through the provision of standardized, leasable services, which can reduce annual costs from as much as CNY 100,000 to as little as CNY 2,000–3,000. The second major benefit of the BSN is its increased level of convenience, which the BSN Development Association believes will encourage greater user participation and the development of new blockchain applications. This increased level of convenience could also lead to a rapid growth in innovation, as a greater number of users will be able to utilize blockchain applications.

Framework and Design of the Digital Yuan

The significant interest in technologies that enable the usage of the digital yuan, as one of the first and most advanced CBDCs, is evident. As previously discussed, different development approaches can be utilized for CBDCs, particularly with regard to user anonymity and the ability for offline transactions. The accessibility of CBDCs can vary widely, as exemplified by the digital euro. China has taken a flexible approach with the digital yuan, allowing for more room for improvement or potential changes based on future technological developments.

It is crucial to understand that the framework of the digital yuan is distinct from that of other privately developed cryptocurrencies. Gantori et al. assert that the only resemblance the digital yuan holds to other cryptocurrencies is that of Facebook's Diem, but these similarities are minimal. The digital yuan's operational framework will be based on a two-tier system, which deviates from the blockchain and consensus protocol mechanisms used by other cryptocurrencies. The digital yuan will be distributed to commercial banks, which will then be responsible for further distribution.

Gantori et al. concur that there is a clear focus on upper-layer issuance and that commercial banks will be able to leverage their technology to issue the currency to consumers. However, commercial banks will still be required to adhere to certain basic requirements.

Table 7.1 illustrates the various components of the digital yuan framework, as determined by the central bank, commercial banks, and end users. It is apparent that the majority of the framework is focused on the central bank, which serves as the issuer and registration authority. The central bank is responsible for overseeing various verifications, registrations, and authorizations, as well as managing liquidity and emergency and error responses. In contrast, commercial banks are delegated with more operational tasks, such as providing customer services like deposit and withdrawal of funds, wallet operations, and error response.

End users are only involved in deposit and withdrawal, and are responsible for logging in, using the currency for payment, and managing payments, as well as utilizing the wallet. In terms of currency retrieval, the central bank assumes responsibility for taking the currency out of circulation, while commercial banks are only responsible for recycling the currency and returning it to end users. The final aspect of the framework (management and control) is overseen by the central bank, which is responsible for ensuring the overall security of the currency, providing fundamental data analysis, and maintaining the currency's well-functioning relationship with commercial banks and end users. Commercial banks have a similar task, but on a smaller scale. The collective aspects of the framework should ensure a well-functioning digital currency at all levels, starting with issuance at the central bank, distribution and customer management at commercial banks, and ultimately use by end users.

Table 7.1: Framework of the digital yuan.

	Issue	Circulation		Management and control		
Central bank	Issue	Ownership verification	Liquidity management	AML (anti-money laundering)	Risk management	Audit
	Register	Transfer registration	Error response	Security	Interconnection	Data analysis
		Authorization management	Emergency response			
Commercial bank	Obtain	Deposit and withdrawal	Wallet	Recycle	Risk management	Data analysis
		Payment	Operation		Security	
		User management	Error response			
End user		Deposit and withdrawal	Log in			
		Pay	Wallet			

Source: Gantori et al. (2020).

Gantori et al. highlight the capacity of the digital yuan, which is noteworthy. The digital yuan is expected to handle 300,000 transactions per second – a significant increase compared to traditional, privately developed cryptocurrencies and current payment systems. The capability for offline transactions is a key point of discussion in relation to the digital yuan. As the digital currency is intended to replicate and potentially replace cash in the future, it must possess similar capabilities to cash.

It is important to note that the digital yuan is not designed as a cryptocurrency. Unlike cryptocurrencies such as Bitcoin and Ethereum, which utilize distributed ledger technology (DLT) to record and store the ownership of coins, the digital yuan uses state-owned databases to record transactions and store ownership data. This also allows the central bank to exert complete control over the currency and transactions.

Benefits of the Digital Yuan

The development and integration of CBDCs by economies such as the EU and China must be justified by the significant benefits that digital currencies offer in offsetting the initial costs in the medium to long term. Gantori et al. have identified three main advantages of the digital yuan, which include a reduction in operational costs, improved supervision and regulation of the currency, and faster growth in digitalization. Additionally, Tran has highlighted the ease of use for consumers as a crucial benefit.

The reduction in operational costs is a significant advantage of the digital yuan. The costs associated with the research and development, printing, and management of the circulation of banknotes and coins are substantial for any economy. Despite the high initial cost, the digital yuan has the potential to help China solve this issue in the long term. Gantori et al. also note the potential for lower costs through the use of smart contracts, which enable autonomous and automatic payments when certain conditions are met, thereby eliminating the need for resources or recurring agreements to conduct such transactions.

The digital yuan also offers improved supervision and regulation of the currency. The digital yuan strikes a balance between controllable anonymity for consumers and classified supervision for the central bank, with potentially less complexity. This approach is believed to enable China to fight against organized crime, money laundering, and corruption more efficiently and effectively, mainly through traceable transactions and the complete replacement of cash with a digital currency. Furthermore, the digital yuan offers consumers the ability to manage their digital identities, which can further strengthen China's implementation and development of new monetary policies.

The digital yuan also facilitates faster growth in terms of digitalization. The rapid development in the digitalization of payments levels the playing field in China, and the introduction of open architecture diminishes the dominance of current tech giants in the e-payment market. As one of the first central banks to advance to the development stage of their CBDC, China also enjoys a first-mover advantage. Finally, Tran highlights the usability of the digital yuan for consumers, noting that transactions can easily be conducted through the scanning of QR codes, using platforms such as Alipay or WeChat Pay. This results in a more effortless and smoother transition away from fiat money.

Cyber and Data Security

There are numerous concerns regarding China's approach to the privacy of transactions and users of the digital yuan. Furthermore, there is a question of how effectively privacy and cybersecurity can coexist. As opposed to physical cash, a patent filed by the People's Bank of China (PCOB) bank suggests that they are exploring a tracking system that would enable the traceability of the digital currency's movements between transactions and individuals. Such traceability could potentially imply little to no privacy for consumers in their transactions. Chinese officials argue that the digital yuan aims to achieve a balance between the two.

These observations may be accurate and align with the objectives set by the Chinese government. Therefore, it is likely that China will endeavor to find the optimal balance between anonymous payments and increased cybersecurity to prevent illegal transactions. To gain a more comprehensive understanding of both areas and their interconnectedness, an analysis of each will be undertaken.

PBOC could acquire enhanced powers of discipline enforcement and would have the ability to take punitive action by blocking transactions, if necessary. Additionally, it would enable them to prohibit purchases of certain goods and currencies, such as gold and US dollars. Tran agrees that such policies fail to provide users with complete anonymity, as is the case with cash transactions.

The drawbacks of implementing complete control over all transactions have been previously outlined. However, China argues that the comprehensive monitoring of transactions is necessary to minimize cyberattack threats. This argument may hold some merit, as Tran and Matthews (2020) states that "the PBoC's ability to monitor DCEP transactions can help improve the efficacy of monetary and fiscal policy operations as well as make it easier to fight financial crimes including money laundering and the financing of terrorism."

However, there is a potential for the government to increase control over citizens even further. China may increase its control to reward or punish the behaviors of digital yuan users. This could pose a potential issue for other central banks planning to develop and issue their own CBDC.

Current State of Digital Yuan

In Suzhou, governmental officials have already begun receiving their transport subsidies in digital currency. Additionally, in Shenzhen, there was a lottery event in October 2020 in which US$1.5 million worth of digital yuan was awarded, with winners able to spend their winnings among 3,000 merchants using a specially developed application on their smartphones. Another extensive trial was conducted in the two largest department stores and one food caterer in Shanghai.

China Construction Bank offered 150 yuan in coupons to 2,000 people making purchases over 380 yuan, with shoppers required to register for an e-wallet trial use at pre-selected branches across Shanghai and download the digital yuan application to their smartphone. Furthermore, the Postal Savings Bank of China developed a special biometric card for trial purposes, allowing participants to quickly identify themselves using only their fingerprint, facilitating the use of the digital yuan and healthcare services for the elderly population.

While other tests and trials of the digital yuan are smaller in scale, Chinese media generally view the development of a sovereign digital currency positively, as it has the potential to revolutionize the ability of regulatory authorities to scrutinize the nation's payment and financial system, granting officials more power to track the use of money by citizens. However, the Chinese public is also aware that the anonymity of transactions may be lost. Foreign economies, particularly the United States, are less favorable towards the digital yuan, with concerns that it could disrupt money and enable the Chinese government to have complete oversight of transactions, thereby strengthening the Chinese Communist Party's digital authoritarianism domestically and exporting its influence and standard-setting abroad. As such, US private sector tech companies are considering whether they will allow the digital yuan application to be accessible on their platforms, such as app stores.

Overall, the development of the digital yuan is in its testing stages and is poised for full release in the near future. The current state of development is positive, with Chinese officials believing that the digital yuan will provide an upper hand over crime and improve currency stability, particularly in extreme events. However, other global economies, particularly the United States, are less favorable towards the digital yuan, raising concerns about its potential impact on the global economy and banking systems.

Chapter Summary

- China was one of the pioneers in the development of CBDCs.
- The digital yuan will be based on China's blockchain service network (BSN).
- The Digital Yuan could also lead to a rapid growth in innovation, as a greater number of users will be able to utilize new blockchain-based applications.
- The People's Bank of China (PBOC) could acquire enhanced powers of discipline enforcement. This would enable them to prohibit purchases of certain goods and currencies, such as gold and US dollars.
- The PBOC's ability to monitor digital yuan transactions can help improve the efficacy of monetary and fiscal policy operations as well as make it easier to fight financial crimes.

Discussion Questions

- How does the digital yuan compare to other digital currencies, such as Bitcoin and Facebook's Diem?
- What are the potential benefits and drawbacks of a digital currency like the digital yuan for consumers and businesses?
- How might the digital yuan affect the global financial system and international trade?
- What are some of the challenges and obstacles facing the widespread adoption of the digital yuan?
- How might the digital yuan impact monetary policy and central banking in China?

- How does the digital yuan fit into the larger context of China's push for greater technological innovation and digitalization?
- How might the digital yuan impact privacy and data security, especially in relation to concerns about the Chinese government's surveillance capabilities?
- What implications might the digital yuan have for the future of cash and physical currency?
- How might other countries respond to the emergence of the digital yuan as a major global currency?
- What opportunities and risks does the digital yuan present for businesses and investors?

Learn from the Web
You can use the following websites to learn more about the digital yuan:

People's Bank of China: http://www.pbc.gov.cn/
The China Center for International Economic Exchanges: http://english.cciee.org.cn/

References

Gantori, S., Hu, Y., Chen, H. & Li, K., (2020). Understanding China's digital currency and blockchain initiatives, s.l.: UBS.

Tran, H., (2020). Can China's digital yuan really challenge the dollar? Atlantic Council. [Online] Available at: https://www.atlanticcouncil.org/blogs/new-atlanticist/can-chinas-digital-yuan-really-challenge-the-dollar/

Yeung, K. (13 May, 2020). What is China's sovereign digital currency? *South China Morning Post*. [Online] Available at: https://www.scmp.com/economy/china-economy/article/3083952/what-chinas-cryptocurrency-sovereign-digital-currency-and-why

Further Reading

Aysan, A. F., & Kayani, F. N. (2022). China's transition to a digital currency does it threaten dollarization? *Asia and the Global Economy, 2*(1), 100023.

Bansal, R., & Singh, S. (2021). China's Digital Yuan: An Alternative to the Dollar-Dominated Financial System. Carnegie Endowment for International Peace.

Kshetri, N. (2023). China's Digital Yuan: Motivations of the Chinese Government and Potential Global Effects. *Journal of Contemporary China, 32*(139), 87–105.

8 Future Research Directions and Concluding Remarks

Introduction

Research on central bank digital currencies (CBDCs) has been more popular in recent years, with more articles examining the potential advantages and difficulties of this novel kind of digital currency. This chapter's goals are to evaluate prior works on CBDCs, pinpoint areas for future research, and suggest a course for CBDC study. With 52 publications published in 2022, an 82% increase from 2021, the use of a Scopus database demonstrated an increasing interest in CBDCs. Nevertheless, despite this expanding interest, there are not many actual CBDCs available right now. To provide a reliable and safe method of trade, it is essential to investigate numerous CBDC features, including potential policy implications and design enhancements. Additionally, the potential impact of CBDCs on the cryptocurrency market and global business must also be examined. Overall, there is a need for further research on CBDCs to fully understand their potential benefits and risks.

Current Research Area on CBDCs

The primary objective of this chapter is to review the trend in past publications on CBDCs to explore research gaps and propose future directions in CBDC research. We used the Scopus database to extract past publications on CBDCs using keywords: central bank digital currency and CBDC. Our initial search provided 196 documents. After reviewing the source title, we removed 87 documents. Next, we extracted "author keywords" from the selected 109 documents and created a word cloud. The word cloud presented in Figure 8.1 clearly reflects the most common keywords in past CBDC studies. Apart from the words embedded in CBDC (central, bank, digital, currency), we find significant presence of the following words in the word cloud: cryptocurrency, blockchain, financial, and system. Table 8.1 presents some of the most frequent words (we only provide words that appear more than 10 times).

https://doi.org/10.1515/9783110982398-008

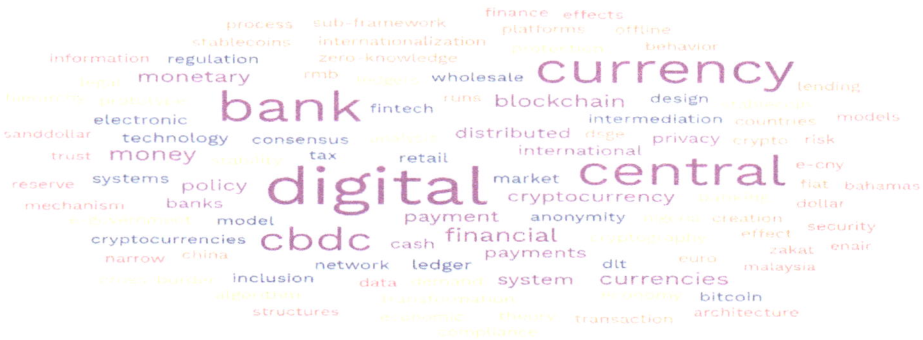

Figure 8.1: The most frequently appearing words in CBDC publications.
Source: Author's own (made using Scopus database)

Table 8.1: Frequency of the most common words in CBDC publications.

Frequency	Word
106	digital
81	bank
81	currency
80	central
57	cbdc
19	financial
19	money
16	currencies
15	blockchain
14	monetary
12	policy
11	payment
11	cryptocurrency
10	system

Source: Author's own (made using Scopus database)

Figure 8.2 indicates the growing popularity of CBDC-related publications. The oldest paper on CBDCs we could find in the Scopus database dates back to 2018. The publication title is Central Banks and Blockchains: The Case for Managing Climate Risk with a Positive Carbon Price by Delton B. Chen. Since 2018, the number of publications on CBDCs has seen an increasing trend, with the total number of papers published in 2022 coming to 52, an 82% increase from 2021. Elsevier has published the highest number of papers on CBDCs, followed by Springer (as shown in Figure 8.3). Of these, 68% are publications in the form of journal articles (see Figure 8.4).

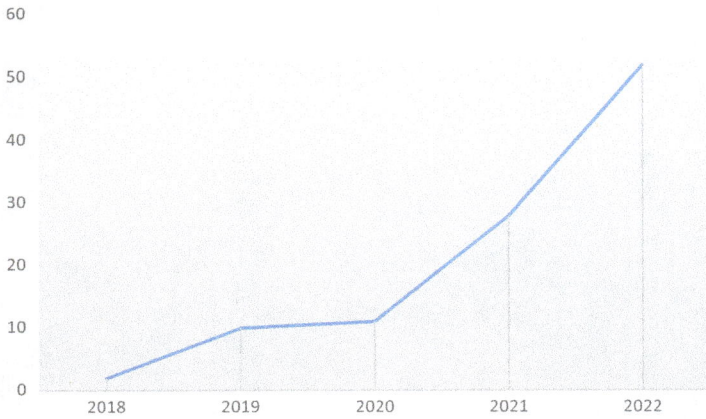

Figure 8.2: Number of publications per year on CBDCs.
Source: Scopus (2023)

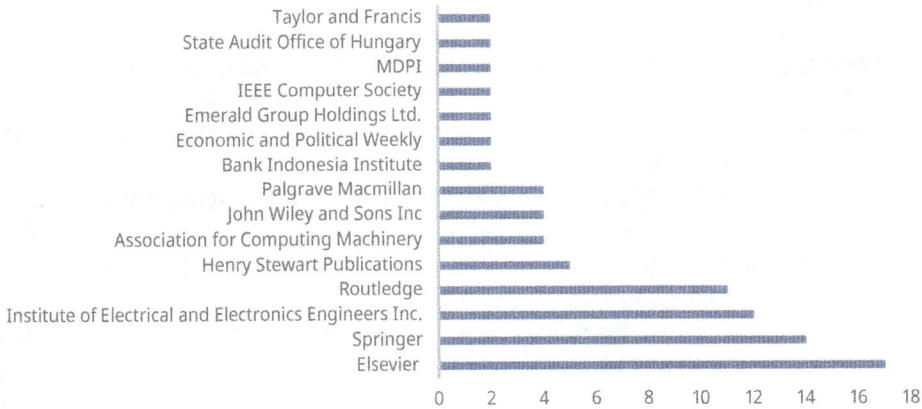

Figure 8.3: Publishers most frequently publishing on CBDCs.
Source: Scopus (2023)

Future Research Directions on CBDCs

After reviewing the past publications on CBDCs, we identified several research questions that could be explored in future research.

1. How will the introduction of CBDCs affect the ability of central banks to conduct monetary policy?
2. How will the introduction of CBDCs affect the use of existing international currencies, such as the US dollar and the euro?

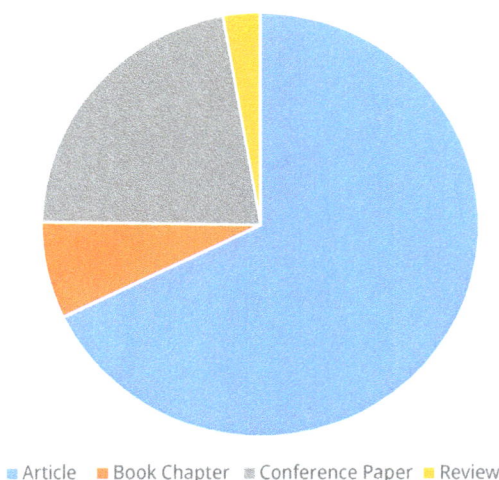

■ Article ■ Book Chapter ■ Conference Paper ■ Review

Figure 8.4: Most common types of publications on CBDC.
Source: Scopus (2023)

3. What implications will this have for international trade and investment?
4. How will CBDCs affect individual privacy and the ability of individuals to access financial services? How can CBDCs be designed to protect privacy while ensuring financial inclusion for all?
5. What are the technical challenges that need to be overcome to implement CBDCs on a large scale?
6. How can CBDCs be scaled to handle the large number of transactions that would be expected in a digital currency system?
7. How will CBDCs affect the ability of governments and financial institutions to detect and prevent illicit financial activities?

Policy Considerations

The ownership and governance model for a cross-border CBDC payment arrangement must be established optimally to comply with relevant regulations. The arrangement should have a transparent and effective governance structure and framework, accommodating stakeholder involvement from multiple central banks, commercial participants, and several other types of actors. While involving stakeholders like central banks increases complexity, it also has benefits such as legitimacy, balance of power, network effects, and alignment of incentives with social welfare. The governance structure should balance sufficient autonomy and control with universality and standardization.

If an error occurs in the selection of the FX rate, the CBDCs must define the allocation of risk among the involved parties clearly and transparently. The FX provider may have an obligation to check that the stipulated exchange rate corresponds to the one posted and be liable for any losses that could arise from an undetected error.

A wallet provider in one country may not know the source of funds sent by a payer in another country in a chain of cross-border payments. CBDCs should maintain a complete log of routed messages and provide services based on a larger information set that can help facilitate the compliance activities of the wallet providers. Central banks developing CBDCs should carefully consider the opportunities to apply new technology and provide services that can help improve the ability of participating institutions to carry out their compliance activities.

Concluding Remarks

CBDCs are a recent innovation in the field of digital currencies that have the potential to revolutionize both individual and corporate payment processes. CBDCs can break the traditional norm of using money. CBDCs are backed by the central bank, which differentiates them from traditional cryptocurrencies. One of the major weaknesses faced by cryptocurrencies is the extent of their instability. CBDCs can improve in terms of stability and risk mitigation with the backing of the central bank. Central banks around the world are experimenting with the concept of a central bank-backed digital currency with a mandate to provide a stable and secure means of exchange. However, there are various challenges which require attention from central banks before the concept of CBDCs can be operationalized.

We do not have enough evidence on the full range of benefits and risks of launching CBDCs. Therefore, there is a need to explore various aspects of CBDCs which could have policy implications and allow central banks to make necessary improvements in the design of CBDCs and the development of relevant regulatory policies to protect the stakeholders. In addition, despite the growing interest in CBDCs, there is currently a lack of actual CBDCs in circulation. This is likely to change in the near future as more and more central banks explore the possibility of issuing their own digital currencies.

One of the most important questions is: Do CBDCs pose a threat to cryptocurrencies? We may need to wait a while to find the answer to this question. However, cryptocurrency providers need to address this threat and find effective ways to prepare for the inevitable launch of CBDCs around the world in the near future.

Finally, we also need to explore the impact of CBDCs on global business. CBDCs have the potential to reshape the way in which business is conducted, and it is important to understand the implications this may have for different industries and business models.

Chapter Summary

- Research on CBDCs has become more popular in recent years.
- The oldest paper on CBDCs we could find in the Scopus database dates back to 2018.
- CBDCs are backed by the central bank, which differentiates them from traditional cryptocurrencies.
- Central banks around the world are experimenting with the concept of a central bank-backed digital currency.
- CBDCs have the potential to reshape the way in which business is conducted.

---

i Learn from the Web

The following resources are useful to explore the latest studies on CBDCs and develop new ideas for research:
- JSTOR: https://www.jstor.org/
- Google Scholar: https://scholar.google.com/
- ResearchGate: https://www.researchgate.net/
- SSRN: https://www.ssrn.com/
- World Scientific: https://www.worldscientific.com/
- Elsevier: https://www.elsevier.com/

References

Scopus (2023). Start exploring. [Online] Available at: https://www.scopus.com/search/form.uri?display=basic#basic

Further Reading

Alfar, A. J., Kumpamool, C., Nguyen, D. T., & Ahmed, R. (2023). The determinants of issuing central bank digital currencies. *Research in International Business and Finance*, *64*, 101884.

Basu, P. (2023). Digital Transformation with CBDC – Genesis, Need and Fundamentals from a Common Man's Perspective. *The Management Accountant Journal*, *58*(1), 74–81.

Gross, M., & Letizia, E. (2023). To Demand or Not to Demand: On Quantifying the Future Appetite for CBDC. Available at: https://www.imf.org/en/Publications/WP/Issues/2023/01/20/To-Demand-or-Not-to-Demand-On-Quantifying-the-Future-Appetite-for-CBDC-528060

Ngo, V. M., Van Nguyen, P., Nguyen, H. H., Tram, H. X. T., & Hoang, L. C. (2023). Governance and monetary policy impacts on public acceptance of CBDC adoption. *Research in International Business and Finance*, *64*, 101865.

Appendix

List of recent papers published on CBDC

Authors	Title	Year
Ozili P. K.	CBDC, Fintech and cryptocurrency for financial inclusion and financial stability	2023
Kaur J.	Central Bank Digital Currency – The 'digital rupee' in India	2023
Tata F.	Proposing an interval design feature to Central Bank Digital Currencies	2023
Camera G.	Introducing New Forms of Digital Money: Evidence from the Laboratory	2023
Ozili P.K.	Central bank digital currency and bank earnings management using loan loss provisions	2023
Rehman M. A., Irfan M., Naeem M. A., Lucey B. M., Karim S.	Macro-financial implications of central bank digital currencies	2023
Alfar A. J. K., Kumpamool C., Nguyen D. T. K., Ahmed R.	The determinants of issuing central bank digital currencies	2023
Tian S., Zhao B., Olivares R. O.	Cybersecurity risks and central banks' sentiment on central bank digital currency: Evidence from global cyberattacks	2023
Sethaput V., Innet S.	Blockchain application for central bank digital currencies (CBDC)	2023
Ngo V. M., Van Nguyen P., Nguyen H. H., Thi Tram H. X., Hoang L. C.	Governance and monetary policy impacts on public acceptance of CBDC adoption	2023
Copestake A., Furceri D., Gonzalez-Dominguez P.	Crypto market responses to digital asset policies	2023
Kuehnlenz S., Orsi B., Kaltenbrunner A.	Central bank digital currencies and the international payment system: The demise of the US dollar?	2023
Jabbar A., Geebren A., Hussain Z., Dani S., Ul-Durar S.	Investigating individual privacy within CBDC: A privacy calculus perspective	2023
Kondova G., Rüegg P.	Central Bank Digital Currencies (CBDCs) as a New Tool of E-Government: Socio-economic Impacts	2023
Zulfikri Z., Sa'ad A. A., Kassim S., Othman A. H. A.	Feasibility of Central Bank Digital Currency for Blockchain-Based Zakat in Indonesia	2023
Awang Abu Bakar N. S., Yahya N., Khairuddin I. E., Zainal Abidin A. F., Mohamad Zain J., Idris N. B., Engku Ali E. R. A.	The Central Bank Digital Currency in Malaysia: A Literature Review	2023

https://doi.org/10.1515/9783110982398-009

(continued)

Authors	Title	Year
Hasan A. K. M. K.	The impact of Central Bank Digital Currency (CBDC) on the operations of Islamic banks	2022
Aneja R., Dygas R.	Digital currencies and the new global financial system	2022
Srouji J., Torre D.	The Global Pandemic, Laboratory of the Cashless Economy?	2022
Park K., Youm H.-Y.	Proposal of Decentralized P2P Service Model for Transfer between Blockchain-Based Heterogeneous Cryptocurrencies and CBDCs	2022
Mzoughi H., Benkraiem R., Guesmi K.	The bitcoin market reaction to the launch of central bank digital currencies	2022
Wang Y.-R., Ma C.-Q., Ren Y.-S.	A model for CBDC audits based on blockchain technology: Learning from the DCEP	2022
Son J., Bilgin M. H., Ryu D.	Consumer choices under new payment methods	2022
Li Z., Yang C., Huang Z.	How does the fintech sector react to signals from central bank digital currencies?	2022
Bhaskar R., Hunjra A. I., Bansal S., Pandey D. K.	Central Bank Digital Currencies: Agendas for future research	2022
Morgan J.	Systemic stablecoin and the defensive case for Central Bank Digital Currency: A critique of the Bank of England's framing	2022
Ding S., Cui T., Wu X., Du M.	Supply chain management based on volatility clustering: The effect of CBDC volatility	2022
Kiayias A., Kohlweiss M., Sarencheh A.	PEReDi: Privacy-Enhanced, Regulated and Distributed Central Bank Digital Currencies	2022
Wüst K., Kostiainen K., Delius N., Capkun S.	Platypus: A Central Bank Digital Currency with Unlinkable Transactions and Privacy-Preserving Regulation	2022
Williamson S.	Central Bank Digital Currency: Welfare and Policy Implications	2022
Kim J. J., Radic A., Chua B.-L., Koo B., Han H.	Digital currency and payment innovation in the hospitality and tourism industry	2022
Scharnowski S.	Central bank speeches and digital currency competition	2022
Oh E. Y., Zhang S.	Informal economy and central bank digital currency	2022
Kwon O., Lee S., Park J.	Central bank digital currency, tax evasion, and inflation tax	2022

(continued)

Authors	Title	Year
Li Z., Zhang Y., Wang Q., Chen S.	Transactional Network Analysis and Money Laundering Behavior Identification of Central Bank Digital Currency of China	2022
Keister T., Monnet C.	Central bank digital currency: Stability and information	2022
Pelagidis T., Kostika E.	Investigating the role of central banks in the interconnection between financial markets and cryptoassets	2022
Davoodalhosseini S. M.	Central bank digital currency and monetary policy	2022
Barrdear J., Kumhof M.	The macroeconomics of central bank digital currencies	2022
Yang J., Zhou G.	A study on the influence mechanism of CBDC on monetary policy: An analysis based on e-CNY	2022
Xu J.	Developments and Implications of Central Bank Digital Currency: The Case of China e-CNY	2022
Wang Y., Lucey B. M., Vigne S. A., Yarovaya L.	The Effects of Central Bank Digital Currencies News on Financial Markets	2022
Koziuk V., Ivashuk Y.	Does it Matter for CBDC Design? Privacy-Anonymity Preferences from the Side of Hierarchies and Egalitarian Cultural Patterns	2022
Xu C., Jin B.	Digital currency in China: pilot implementations, legal challenges and prospects	2022
Huang Y., Mayer M.	Digital currencies, monetary sovereignty, and US–China power competition	2022
Oehler-Șincai I. M.	The Digital Euro Project. A Preliminary Assessment	2022
Castrén O., Kavonius I. K., Rancan M.	Digital currencies in financial networks	2022
Allen F., Gu X., Jagtiani J.	Fintech, Cryptocurrencies, and CBDC: Financial Structural Transformation in China	2022
Chen H., Siklos P. L.	Central bank digital currency: A review and some macro-financial implications	2022
Zhang T., Huang Z.	Blockchain and central bank digital currency	2022
Tronnier F., Harborth D., Hamm P.	Investigating privacy concerns and trust in the digital Euro in Germany	2022
Syarifuddin F., Bakhtiar T.	The Macroeconomic Effects of an Interest-Bearing CBDC: A DSGE Model	2022

(continued)

Authors	Title	Year
Chu Y., Lee J., Kim S., Kim H., Yoon Y., Chung H.	Review of Offline Payment Function of CBDC Considering Security Requirements	2022
Pocher N., Zichichi M.	Towards CBDC-based machine-to-machine payments in consumer IoT	2022
Ferrari Minesso M., Mehl A., Stracca L.	Central bank digital currency in an open economy	2022
Kim B., Kim H. J., Lee J.	First Smart Contract Allowing Cryptoasset Recovery	2022
Ray P., Saha D., Unni V. K.	The Union Budget and the Central Bank Digital Currency: Speculating on the Shape of Things to Come	2022
Bolt W., Lubbersen V., Wierts P.	Getting the balance right: Crypto, stablecoin and central bank digital currency	2022
Cheng J., Torregrossa J.	What is money? A lawyer's perspective on the evolution of the US payment system and dollars in the digital age	2022
Fegatelli P.	A central bank digital currency in a heterogeneous monetary union: Managing the effects on the bank lending channel	2022
Cullen J.	"Economically inefficient and legally untenable": constitutional limitations on the introduction of central bank digital currencies in the EU	2022
Dupuis D., Gleason K., Wang Z.	Money laundering in a CBDC world: a game of cats and mice	2022
Ortino M.	The Functions of Law and of Digital Platforms in the Payment System	2022
Kesavaraj S. V., Jakhiya C. M., Bhandari C. N.	A Study on Upcoming Central Bank Digital Currency: Opportunities, Obstacles, and Potential FinTech Solutions using Cryptography in the Indian Scenario	2022
Terták E., Kovács L.	The Motives for Issuing Central Bank Digital Currency and the Challenges of Introduction Thereof	2022
Boros E., Horváth M.	Central Bank Digital Currency: the Next Money Revolution?	2022
Yang B., Zhang Y., Tong D.	DOT-M: A Dual Offline Transaction Scheme of Central Bank Digital Currency for Trusted Mobile Devices	2022
Buldas A., Draheim D., Saarepera M.	Secure and Efficient Implementation of Electronic Money	2022
Jagrič T., Fister D., Amon A., Jagrič V., Beloglavec S. T.	The Banking Industry in the Ecosystem of Digital Currencies and Digital Central Bank Currencies	2022

(continued)

Authors	Title	Year
Tsindeliani I., Anisina K., Babayan O., Bit-Shabo I., Kostikova E., Migacheva E.	Digitalising the state monetary system: national implementation model	2022
Islam M. M., IN H. P.	A Privacy-Preserving Transparent Central Bank Digital Currency System Based on Consortium Blockchain and Unspent Transaction Outputs	2022
Li J.	Predicting the demand for central bank digital currency: A structural analysis with survey data	2022
Ren D., Guo H., Jiang T.	Managed anonymity of CBDC, social welfare and taxation: A new monetarist perspective	2022
Pavoor A. S., Ajithkumar N.	Digital rupee – A rival for cryptos?	2022
Krylova L. V., Lukashenko I. V.	Cryptocurrencies vs Central Banks' Digital Currencies: The Role of Financial Literacy	2022
Koshelev K. A.	Trends in the Evolution of the Digital Financial Assets Market in the Context of the Digital Transformation of the Global Economy	2022
Ozili P. K.	Central bank digital currency in Nigeria: opportunities and risks	2022
Pocher N., Veneris A.	Central Bank Digital Currencies	2022
Singh S., Gupta S., Kaur S., Sapra S., Kumar V., Sharma M.	The quest for CBDC: identifying and prioritising the motivations for launching central bank digital currencies in emerging countries	2022
Dinh H. T. L., Dinh T. C.	Verification of the Impact of Central Bank Digital Currency (CBDC) Issuance on Net Interest Income of Vietnamese Commercial Banks	2022
Udalov I., Abdimomynova A., Moldagulova S.	Multifractal and Cross-correlation Analysis of Cryptocurrencies for Direct Green Investments	2022
Dai Y.	Business Cycle Synchronization and Multilateral Trade Integration in the BRICS	2022
Bagis B.	Digital Currencies and Monetary Policy in the New Era	2022
Liu X., Wang Q., Wu G., Zhang C.	Determinants of individuals' intentions to use central bank digital currency: evidence from China	2022
Wang G., Hausken K.	A game between central banks and households involving central bank digital currencies, other digital currencies and negative interest rates	2022

(continued)

Authors	Title	Year
Abu N. A.	Keynote Paper Digital Ringgit: A New Digital Currency with Traditional Attributes	2022
Liu Y., Ni J., Zulkernine M.	AT-CBDC: Achieving Anonymity and Traceability in Central Bank Digital Currency	2022
Babin R., Smith D., Shah H.	Central bank digital currency: Advising the financial services industry	2022
Auer R., Frost J., Gambacorta L., Monnet C., Rice T., Shin H. S.	Central Bank Digital Currencies: Motives, Economic Implications, and the Research Frontier	2022
Maryaningsih N., Nazara S., Kacaribu F. N., Juhro S. M.	Central Bank Digital Currency: What Factors Determine Its Adoption?	2022
Franko A., Olah B., Sass Z., Hegedus C., Varga P.	Towards CBDC-supported Smart Contracts for Industrial Stakeholders	2022
Polivach A. P.	Digital Rouble and Prospects of Russian Currency's Internationalisation	2022
Semeko G. V.	Sovereign Digital Currency – A New Reality	2022
Ozturkcan S., Senel K., Ozdinc M.	Framing the Central Bank Digital Currency (CBDC) revolution	2022
Sidorenko E. L., Khisamova Z. I., Inozemtsev M. I., Von Arx P.	Digital Ruble: Assessing the Criminological Risks of the Proposed Model	2022
Jin S. Y., Xia Y.	CEV Framework: A Central Bank Digital Currency Evaluation and Verification Framework with a Focus on Consensus Algorithms and Operating Architectures	2022
Fleming M., King A., Parr F.	Enterprise Payments with Central Bank Digital Currency: An End-to-End Technology Point of View	2022
Brunnhuber S.	The Real Tragedy of the Commons – Garrett Hardin (1968) Revised	2022
Luu H. N., Do D. D., Pham T., Ho V. X., Dinh Q.-A.	Cultural values and the adoption of central bank digital currency	2022
Slawotsky J.	Digital currencies and great power rivalry: China as a disseminator in the digital age	2022
Shelepov A.	The Influence of the G20's Digitalization Leadership on Development Conditions and Governance of the Digital Economy	2022

(continued)

Authors	Title	Year
Radic A., Quan W., Koo B., Chua B.-L., Kim J. J., Han H.	Central bank digital currency as a payment method for tourists: application of the theory of planned behavior to Digital Yuan/Won/Dollar choice	2022
Didenko A. N., Buckley R. P.	Central bank digital currencies as a potential response to some particularly Pacific problems	2022
Bindseil U.	Central Bank Digital Currencies in a World with Negative Nominal Interest Rates	2022
Cheng P.	Decoding the rise of central bank digital currency in China: designs, problems, and prospects	2022
Jozipović Š., Perkušić M., Gadžo S.	Tax Compliance in the Era of Cryptocurrencies and CBDCs: The End of the Right to Privacy or No Reason for Concern?	2022
Mooij A. M.	A digital euro for everyone: Can the European System of Central Banks introduce general purpose CBDC as part of its economic mandate?	2022
Kim Y. S., Kwon O.	Central Bank Digital Currency, Credit Supply, and Financial Stability	2022
Ozili P. K.	Central bank digital currency research around the world: a review of literature	2022
Mello G. M. C., Nakatani P., Wong E.	Dollar Hegemony Under Challenge and the Rise of Central Bank Digital Currencies (CBDC): A New Form of World Money?	2022
Wilkins C. A.	Discussion of "designing central bank digital currency" by Agur, Ari and Dell'Ariccia	2022
Agur I., Ari A., Dell'Ariccia G.	Designing central bank digital currencies	2022
Peneder M.	Digitization and the evolution of money as a social technology of account	2022
Dostov V., Pimenov P., Shoust P., Krivoruchko S., Titov V.	Comparison of the Digital Ruble Concept with Foreign Central Bank Digital Currencies	2021
Jun J., Yeo E.	Central bank digital currency, loan supply, and bank failure risk: a microeconomic approach	2021
Laboure M., H.-P. Müller M., Heinz G., Singh S., Köhling S.	Cryptocurrencies and CBDC: The Route Ahead	2021
Lee Y., Son B., Jang H., Byun J., Yoon T., Lee J.	Atomic cross-chain settlement model for central banks digital currency	2021

(continued)

Authors	Title	Year
Bian W., Ji Y., Wang P.	The crowding-out effect of central bank digital currencies: A simple and generalizable payment portfolio model	2021
Bhawana, Kumar S.	Permission Blockchain Network based Central Bank Digital Currency	2021
Kochergin D. A.	Modern models of systems of central bank digital currency	2021
Ashurst S., Tempesta S.	Blockchain applied: Practical technology and use cases of enterprise blockchain for the real world	2021
Han J., Kim J., Youn A., Lee J., Chun Y., Woo J., Hong J. W.-K.	Cos-CBDC: Design and Implementation of CBDC on Cosmos Blockchain	2021
Zellweger-Gutknecht C., Geva B., Grünewald S. N.	Digital Euro, Monetary Objects, and Price Stability: A Legal Analysis	2021
Ballaschk D., Paulick J.	The public, the private and the secret: Thoughts on privacy in central bank digital currencies	2021
Hernández Fernández F.	Towards a European digital currency. The euro 2.0	2021
Adams M., Boldrin L., Ohlhausen R., Wagner E.	An integrated approach for electronic identification and central bank digital currencies	2021
Lee Y., Son B., Park S., Lee J., Jang H.	A survey on security and privacy in blockchain-based central bank digital currencies	2021
Cunha P. R., Melo P., Sebastião H.	From bitcoin to central bank digital currencies: Making sense of the digital money revolution	2021
Shen W., Hou L.	China's central bank digital currency and its impacts on monetary policy and payment competition: Game changer or regulatory toolkit?	2021
Fernández-Villaverde J., Sanches D., Schilling L., Uhlig H.	Central bank digital currency: Central banking for all?	2021
Meaning J., Dyson B., Barker J., Clayton E.	Broadening narrow money: Monetary policy with a central bank digital currency	2021
Kshetri N.	The Economics of Central Bank Digital Currency	2021
Wagner E., Bruggink D., Benevelli A.	Preparing euro payments for the future: A blueprint for a digital euro	2021
Wang G., Hausken K.	Governmental taxation of households choosing between a national currency and a cryptocurrency	2021
Kochergin D. A.	Central banks digital currencies: World experience	2021

(continued)

Authors	Title	Year
Jung H., Jeong D.	Blockchain implementation method for interoperability between CBDCs	2021
Li D., Wong W. E., Pan S., Koh L. S., Chau M.	Design principles and best practices of central bank digital currency	2021
Fernández M. A. E., Alonso S. L. N., Jorge-Vázquez J., Forradellas R. F. R.	Central banks' monetary policy in the face of the COVID-19 economic crisis: Monetary stimulus and the emergence of CBDCs	2021
Sidorenko E.	Digital currency of central banks economic scenarios and forecasts	2021
McLaughlin T.	Two paths to tomorrow's money	2021
Alonso S. L. N., Jorge-Vazquez J., Forradellas R. F. R.	Central banks digital currency: Detection of optimal countries for the implementation of a CBDC and the implication for payment industry open innovation	2021
Sanchez-Roger M., Puyol-Antón E.	Digital bank runs: A deep neural network approach	2021
Koziuk V.	Confidence in digital money: Are central banks more trusted than age is matter?	2021
Crawford J., Menand L., Ricks M.	FedAccounts: Digital Dollars	2021
Shelepov A.	Regulating Global Stablecoins and Central Bank Digital Currencies In Selected G20 Countries	2021
Sethaput V., Innet S.	Blockchain Application for Central Bank Digital Currencies (CBDC)	2021
Geva B., Grünewald S. N., Zellweger-Gutknecht C.	The e-Banknote as a 'Banknote': A Monetary Law Interpreted	2021
Nechitailo V., Penikas H.	Agent-based modeling for benchmarking banking regulation regimes: Application for the CBDC	2021
Rennie E., Steele S.	Privacy and Emergency Payments in a Pandemic: How to Think about Privacy and a Central Bank Digital Currency	2021
Jiang J., Lyu A.	A Game Model for Incentive Mechanism of Distributed Nodes in Supply Chains	2021
Arauz A.	The International Hierarchy of Money in Cross-Border Payment Systems: Developing Countries' Regulation for Central Bank Digital Currencies and Facebook's Stablecoin	2021
Samek M., Vlasta M.	Digital Yuan – Currency or Policy Tool?	2021

(continued)

Authors	Title	Year
Scarcella L.	The Implications of Adopting a European Central Bank Digital Currency: A Tax Policy Perspective	2021
Slim A.	Will the BRICS be the leaders in central bank digital currencies?	2021
Tronnier F.	Privacy in Payment in the Age of Central Bank Digital Currency	2021
Mou C., Tsai W.-T., Jiang X., Yang D.	Game-Theoretic Analysis on CBDC Adoption	2021
Mikhaylov A. Y.	Development of Friedrich von Hayek's theory of private money and economic implications for digital currencies	2021
Zhang J., Tian R., Cao Y., Yuan X., Yu Z., Yan X., Zhang X.	A Hybrid Model for Central Bank Digital Currency Based on Blockchain	2021
Amaral G., Sales T. P., Guizzardi G.	Towards ontological foundations for central bank digital currencies	2021
Tong W., Jiayou C.	A study of the economic impact of central bank digital currency under global competition	2021
Lee D. K. C., Yan L., Wang Y.	A global perspective on central bank digital currency	2021
Li S., Huang Y.	The genesis, design and implications of China's central bank digital currency	2021
Chorzempa M.	China, the United States, and central bank digital currencies: how important is it to be first?	2021
Sidorenko E. L., Sheveleva S. V., Lykov A. A.	Legal and Economic Implications of Central Bank Digital Currencies (CBDC)	2021
Xu Z., Zou C.	What can blockchain do and cannot do?	2021
Zhang X.	Opportunities, challenges and promotion countermeasures of central bank digital currency	2020
Sartori L.	Complementary or substitutive, public or private: The differentiation process of money	2020
Nabilou H.	Testing the waters of the Rubicon: the European Central Bank and central bank digital currencies	2020
Sasongko D. T., Yazid S.	Integrated DLT and non-DLT system design for central bank digital currency	2020
Viñuela C., Sapena J., Wandosell G.	The Future of Money and the Central Bank Digital Currency Dilemma	2020

(continued)

Authors	Title	Year
Zams B. M., Indrastuti R., Pangersa A. G., Hasniawati N. A., Zahra F. A., Fauziah I. A.	Designing central bank digital currency for Indonesia: The delphi-analytic network process	2020
Selim M.	Countercyclical monetary policy for overcoming COVID-19 induced recession by introducing incentive based digital currency	2020
Belke A., Beretta E.	From cash to private and public digital currencies: The risk of financial instability and "modern monetary middle ages"	2020
Alonso S. L. N., Jorge-Vazquez J., Forradellas R. F. R.	Detection of financial inclusion vulnerable rural areas through an access to cash index: Solutions based on the pharmacy network and a CBDC. Evidence based on Ávila (Spain)	2020
Cukierman A.	Reflections on welfare and political economy aspects of a central bank digital currency	2020
Alonso S. L. N., Fernández M.Á.E., Bas D. S., Kaczmarek J.	Reasons Fostering or Discouraging the Implementation of Central Bank-Backed Digital Currency: A Review	2020
Sempere C. P.	The digitalisation of money and payments in the post-COVID digital market economy	2020
Kochergin D., Dostov V.	Central Banks Digital Currency: Issuing and Integration Scenarios in the Monetary and Payment System	2020
Dai W., Gu X., Teng Y.	A Supervised Anonymous Issuance Scheme of Central Bank Digital Currency Based on Blockchain	2020
Liu C.-Y., Hou C.-C.	A research on blockchain-based central bank digital currency	2020
Dashkevich N., Counsell S., Destefanis G.	Blockchain Application for Central Banks: A Systematic Mapping Study	2020
Tronnier F., Recker M., Hamm P.	Towards Central Bank Digital Currency – A Systematic Literature Review	2020
Opare E. A., Kim K.	A Compendium of Practices for Central Bank Digital Currencies for Multinational Financial Infrastructures	2020
Sinelnikova-Muryleva E. V.	Central bank digital currencies: Potential risks and benefits	2020
Fonseca G.	An analysis of the legal impact of central bank digital currency on the European payments landscape	2019
Han X., Yuan Y., Wang F.-Y.	A Blockchain-based Framework for Central Bank Digital Currency	2019

(continued)

Authors	Title	Year
Cao Y., Zhang J., Yuan X., Guo T., Lu C., Chen G., Kang J., Yan X., Zhang X., Huang Y.	A hybrid blockchain system based on parallel distributed architecture for central bank digital currency	2019
Bindseil U.	Central Bank Digital Currency: Financial System Implications and Control	2019
Brunnermeier M. K., Niepelt D.	On the equivalence of private and public money	2019
Hamza H., Ben Jedidia K.	Central bank digital currency and financial stability in a dual banking system	2019
Gopane T. J.	An Enquiry into Digital Inequality Implications for Central Bank Digital Currency	2019
Karamollaoglu N., Tuncay B.	New money: Central bank digital currencies	2019
Khiaonarong T., Humphrey D.	Cash use across countries and the demand for central bank digital currency	2019
Qian Y.	Central bank digital currency: optimization of the currency system and its issuance design	2019
Kochergin D. A., Yangirova A. I.	Central bank digital currencies: Key characteristics and directions of influence on monetary and credit and payment systems	2019
Bystryakov A., Nenovsky N., Ponomarenko E.	Monetary innovations and digital economy	2019
Sławiński A.	Could cryptocurrencies or CBDCs replace the recent monetary systems?	2019
Tsai W.-T., Zhao Z., Zhang C., Yu L., Deng E.	A multi-chain model for CBDC	2018
Yao Q.	Experimental Study on Prototype System of Central Bank Digital Currency	2018
Chen D. B.	Central Banks and Blockchains: The Case for Managing Climate Risk With a Positive Carbon Price	2018
Ben Dhaou S. I., Rohman I. K.	Everything and its opposite: Socio-economic implications of Blockchain technology: Case of monetary policy	2018
Sun H., Mao H., Bai X., Chen Z., Hu K., Yu W.	Multi-Blockchain Model for Central Bank Digital Currency	2018
Chen D. B.	Central Banks and Blockchains: The Case for Managing Climate Risk with a Positive Carbon Price	2018

List of Figures

https://doi.org/10.1515/9783110982398-010

List of Tables

https://doi.org/10.1515/9783110982398-011

About the Authors

Muhammad Ashfaq is a professor of finance and accounting and Academic Director International at the IU International University of Applied Sciences in Germany. He is also visiting professor at Wittenborg University of Applied Sciences in the Netherlands. His research interests include sustainable finance, digital transformation, FinTech, emerging markets, and AI's role in the financial system. He earned his doctoral degree on the topic of knowledge, attitude, and practices toward Islamic banking and finance from the University of Tübingen. He also received an MBA in financial management from Coburg University. Mr. Ashfaq has played a key role in the conceptualization, development, and accreditation of study programs in various countries. He has most recently developed an extensive and innovative bachelor's degree program in digital business and M.Sc. Finance, Accounting & Taxation at IU International University.

Rashedul Hasan is an accomplished lecturer in accounting at Coventry University, based in the United Kingdom. Dr. Hasan began his academic career in 2011. He completed his PhD in 2018, with a research focus on corporate governance issues for non-profit organizations. Dr. Hasan is also a CIMA member, having earned the prestigious designation of ACMA, CGMA. As a researcher, Dr. Hasan's interests lie in the areas of corporate governance dynamics, FinTech, performance and risk management aspects of financial institutions, as well as sustainability and accountability issues. He has been serving as the associate editor of the Quarterly Journal of Finance and Accounting, the International Journal of Islamic and Middle Eastern Finance and Management, and the Journal of Economic Cooperation and Development, which is a testament to his academic prowess and exceptional editorial skills. Dr. Hasan regularly publishes his research in ABS, ABDC, and SCOPUS indexed accounting and finance journals.

Jošt Merčon is currently working as a finance manager at Gamanza Group AG in Ljubljana, Slovenia. He previously worked as a senior audit analyst and audit assistant at Deloitte in Slovenia. Merčon holds a master's degree in international management with a major in finance and accounting from IU International University of Applied Sciences.

https://doi.org/10.1515/9783110982398-012

Index

https://doi.org/10.1515/9783110982398-013

www.ingramcontent.com/pod-product-compliance
Lightning Source LLC
Chambersburg PA
CBHW081517190326
41458CB00015B/5391